A Guide to FAMILY-CENTERED CIRCLE DRAWINGS (F-C-C-D) with Symbol Probes and Visual Free Association

Other Books by Robert C. Burns

KINETIC FAMILY DRAWINGS (K-F-D)
(with S. H. Kaufman) (1970)

ACTIONS, STYLES AND SYMBOLS
IN KINETIC FAMILY DRAWINGS (K-F-D)
(with S. H. Kaufman) (1972)

SELF-GROWTH IN FAMILIES
Kinetic Family Drawings (K-F-D)
Research and Application (1982)

KINETIC-HOUSE-TREE-PERSON DRAWINGS (K-H-T-P)
An Interpretative Manual (1987)

A Guide to FAMILY-CENTERED CIRCLE DRAWINGS (F-C-C-D) with Symbol Probes and Visual Free Association

ROBERT C. BURNS

Seattle Institute of Human Development

BRUNNER/MAZEL PUBLISHERS · NEW YORK

Library of Congress Cataloging-in-Publication Data
Burns, Robert C.
A guide to family-centered circle drawings (F-C-C-D) with symbol probes and visual free association / by Robert C. Burns.
p. cm.
Includes bibliographical references.
ISBN 0-87630-587-7
1. Family-Centered Circle Drawings. 2. Free association (psychology) 3. Mental illness—Diagnosis. 4. Psychotherapy. I. Title.
[DNLM: 1. Art. 2. Family. 3. Personality Tests—methods. 4. Symbolism (Psychology) 5. Visual Perception. BF 698.8.D68 B967g]
RC473.F35B87 1990
616.89'075—dc20
DNLM/DLC
for Library of Congress 90-1935
CIP

Published by
BRUNNER/MAZEL, INC.
19 Union Square West
New York, New York 10003

Manufactured in the United States of America

10 9 8 7 6 5 4 3 2 1

CONTENTS

Preface vii

1. GETTING IN TOUCH WITH YOUR INNER PARENTS 1

Mandalas 1
Symmetry and Centering 2
Inner Parents 3
Family-Centered Circle Drawings 3
Instructions for Obtaining a Family-Centered Circle Drawing 3
Parents-Self-Centered Drawings 10
Instructions for Obtaining a Parents-Self Centered Drawing 10
Symbol-Centered Probe 12
Instructions for Obtaining a Symbol-Centered Probe 12

2. FAMILY-CENTERED CIRCLE DRAWINGS (F-C-C-D) 20

Verbal Free Association 20
Sign and Symbol Systems in Healing 20
Visual Free Association in the F-C-C-D 21
Some Things to Look for in an F-C-C-D 21

3. PARENTS-SELF-CENTERED CIRCLE DRAWINGS (P-S-C-D) . . . 108

Internal and External Parents and Self 108
Some Things to Look for in a P-S-C-D 108
Instructions for Obtaining a P-S-C-D 109
Moons as Symbols of Depression 124

4. SYMBOL-CENTERED PROBES (SYM-C-P) AND DOODLE PROBES 154

5. THE CENTERING PROCESS AS SHOWN IN KINETIC DRAWINGS 166

Instructions for Obtaining a Kinetic-Shop-Window Drawing 167
Instructions for Obtaining a Kinetic-House-Tree-Person Drawing 167
Maria's Centering Journey 168

6. CONCLUSIONS 180

Qualities Seen in Unhealthy Internalized Parents and Self Drawings 181
Specific Omission or Overemphasis in F-C-C-Ds 181
Overemphasis 182
Qualities Seen in Healthy Internalized Parents and Self Drawings 182

Appendix: Frequent Symbols in Kinetic and Family Circle Drawings 189

References 193

Additional Readings 195

PREFACE

Seeing ourselves in relation to our inner parents is the focal point of this book. By drawing a picture, of each of our parents alone, of our self alone, and of both parents with the self in a circle-centered drawing, we begin to see parent-self relationships more clearly.

By drawing symbols or doodles around the circle, we uncover distilled ideas and emotions condensed in these symbols. By centering some of these symbols and then surrounding them with a fresh circle of symbols, a "symbol probe" is used to penetrate more deeply into the unconscious.

The history of human figure drawings as psychological probing devices is short. In this country, Florence Goodenough (1926) created the Draw-A-Person test. A single human figure drawing was scored for individual characteristics. The summary score was viewed as an intelligence quotient and correlated with I.Q. tests.

Clinicians like Karen Machover (1949) saw personality characteristics in the human figure drawings and focused on these characteristics as a means to better understand emotional aspects of the drawer.

Some 20 years ago, kinetic aspects were introduced into human figure drawings by Burns and Kaufman (1970, 1972, 1982). The drawer was asked to add movement to family drawings. When action was added to the drawings, new dimensions were revealed. Actions and interactions of and between the human figures revealed dynamics not seen in akinetic drawing techniques. Kinetic drawings of individuals and families, even of trees and houses and people (Burns, 1987), became a new area of study.

The "idea" for gathering kinetic drawings was inspired by Anaxagoras of Clazomenae (500-428 B.C.). Few are as familiar with the works (mostly fragments) of Anaxagoras as they are with his student Socrates or with those of Socrates' student, Plato. Most of us know Socrates drank poisonous hemlock, but few know he was forced to drink hemlock for espousing the views of Anaxagoras.

Ionian science was introduced into Athens by Anaxagoras who was the first philosopher to take up his residence in Athens, which was then making itself, under the leadership of Pericles, the most prominent city in Greece (Scoon, 1928).

Among the Greeks, Anaxagoras was known as Ho Nous (The Understanding). Anaxagoras defined Understanding (Nous) as "giving movement, unity and system to what had previously been a jumble of inert elements."

In my field of projective drawings of human figures, the figures had been treated as "inert elements." Through the inspiration of Anaxagoras, I introduced movement into human drawings as a projective drawing technique, that is, *Kinetic Family Drawings* (Burns & Kaufman, 1970).

Looking for further inspiration, I turned to the East with its emphasis on circle drawings and Mandalas as techniques for focusing and inner growth. The printed word in the West tends to be linear and fragmented. In contrast, oriental ideograms are holistic and visual. Ideograms are more than isolated individual words; they are symbols portraying condensed wisdom. Consider the Chinese ideogram for "listen."

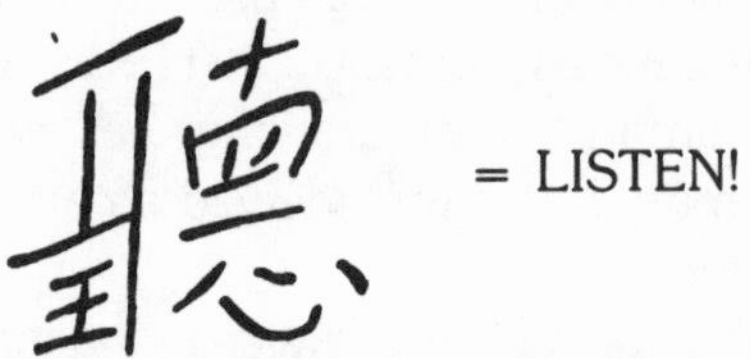

How beautiful and challenging to hear-see-feel the parts of the listen-symbol as it blends into a harmonious whole:

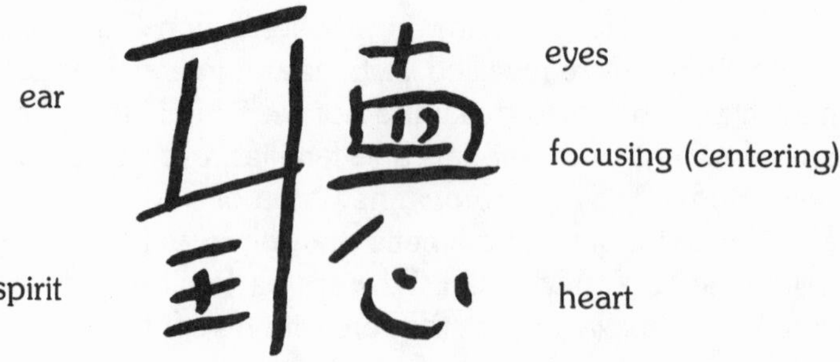

How wonderful if therapists could focus the ears, eyes and heart in "listening" in a therapeutic relationship.

I think of the wonderful therapists I have known such as Abraham Maslow and Carl Rogers—how they listened with the heart! and the eye—and the ear—the complete "therapist-healer."

Herman Rorschach (1942), one of the originators of psychological projective techniques, did much inkblot research before formally introducing his inkblot test. In his experimental work, Rorschach found that inkblots which were symmetrical produced more responses and more unconscious material than asymmetrical inkblots.

Utilizing Rorschach's findings related to increased projective material with *symmetry* and the concept of centering symbols a new drawing technique is offered: Family-Centered Circle Drawings (F-C-C-D). Individual family members are centered in a circular (symmetrical) matrix. The central figure is surrounded by symbols drawn around the periphery of the circle, that is, *visually free associated.*

When one places a symbol drawn around the periphery in the center of a new drawing and visually free associates around it, a Symbol-Centered Probe (SYM-C-P) is obtained. We will try to show how these SYM-C-Ps may be used in a variety of ways to tap into the unconscious and uncover positive and negative energy systems (symbols).

This book reflects an attempt to help healers "listen" to the visual communications of the drawer. We can train ourselves to "listen" with the ear and eye. "Listening" with the heart may also be taught someday.

I thank my children, Heather and Carter, for their love, patience and skill in helping me to prepare this manuscript. Thanks also to Kathleen Provazek for her helpful comments, and to Sara Porter for her art work.

Thanks, also, to the drawers who graciously shared their pictures with us and thereby helped us to grow.

Chapter 1

GETTING IN TOUCH WITH YOUR INNER PARENTS

This book provides an opportunity to introduce a new projective drawing technique called Family-Centered Circle Drawings (F-C-C-D). This technique helps people get in touch with their inner parents and self. One way to get in touch with inner parents is by talking "about" them using a sign system, that is, words. Freud had people talk about themselves and free associate to childhood memories.

Many people have spent many hours and years lying on a couch talking and having a Freudian analyst analyze the words. This process is very slow, restricted to one sign system, and costly. Freud's methods using verbal free association and talking analysis have become a model for psychotherapy in the west.

Another way to "get in touch with" parents is through drawings, that is, *symbol systems.* In contrast to sign systems, which are created by someone else, symbol systems are created by individuals. Thus, symbol systems can bring us closer to our center.

MANDALAS

Jung studied Mandalas from eastern cultures. A Mandala is essentially a centered symbol in a symmetrical design.

Centered in these Mandalas was usually some object or symbol considered holy or inspirational or balancing. The relationship of Jung's work to eastern thought from which the Mandala concept was taken is discussed by Coward

(1985). Jung credited his studies of Mandalas and centering as most beneficial in his own search for balance and health.

SYMMETRY AND CENTERING

Symmetry

Herman Rorschach (1942) did much research with various inkblot patterns before formally introducing his inkblot test in 1921. His experimental research indicated that symmetrical inkblots produced more responses and more unconscious material than asymmetrical inkblots. By placing our family figures in the center of a circle, we adhere to Rorschach's suggestion for increasing projective material.

Centering

Some years ago, California publisher Stewart Brand took the one million dollars in profits from *The Whole Earth Catalogue* and launched an unusual talent search. His goal; to give away this money to the California bay area's most gifted and creative individuals.

Michael Phillips—the investment banker who created Mastercharge—helped Brand by selecting over 100 artists, scientists, poets, and social innovators. He asked these candidates to name the single most important influence on their own life's work. An astounding number—more than half—referred to M. C. Richards and her book, *Centering* (Richards, 1962). Richards had been a faculty member in the English department at the University of California who gave up teaching to become a potter. She had been influenced by Paul Reps's centering discussion in *Zen Flesh, Zen Bones* (1957). It was the potters wheel that provided Richards with her most powerful metaphor for transformation. Centering, she said, is a task as essential to the making of a person as it is to the throwing of clay pots.

By centering a symbol and focusing upon it in a symmetrical matrix, one may elicit deep emotional reaction. In the religious world focusing upon centered symbols such as a cross, star, lamb, divine figure, and so on may bring insights and healing. In the projective drawing world, centering upon the self-created images of the parents or of the parents and the self may also bring insights and healing.

INNER PARENTS

Throughout this book we will see drawings showing how people feel about their inner parents. Do they touch their parents? Do they abhor their parents and refuse to be near them? Do they create barriers between themselves and their parents? Do the parents see? Do the parents care?

Fascinating information about the family is obtained through the use of centered symmetrical drawing techniques.

In this chapter, we see and discuss four types of Family-Centered Circle Drawings (F-C-C-D): (1) Mother-Centered; (2) Father-Centered; (3) Self-Centered; and (4) Parents-Self-Centered. Symbol-Centered Probes (SYM-C-P) may be used to explore any symbols appearing in the F-C-C-Ds.

FAMILY-CENTERED CIRCLE DRAWINGS

Instructions for Obtaining a Family-Centered Circle Drawing

When we place the mother, father, or self in the center of a circle and visually free associate around the periphery, we obtain a Family-Centered Circle Drawing.

The drawer is given a standard sheet of typing paper ($8\frac{1}{2} \times 11$ inches) with a circle already drawn on the paper with a diameter of $7\frac{1}{2}$ to 9 inches. The diameter may vary as the diameter of heads vary. The instructions for obtaining an F-C-C-D are: *"Draw your mother in the center of a circle. Visually free associate with drawn symbols around the periphery of the circle. Try to draw a whole person, not a stick or cartoon figure."*

These instructions are repeated, substituting father and self for mother. Three separate drawings are obtained. Following are examples of F-C-C-Ds.

Drawing 1. CAROL'S F-C-C-D: FATHER-CENTERED

The symbols surrounding the father might be divided into music, books, sports and travel. Usually symbols on top are most significant i.e., music and books. The Eiffel tower full of "X"s (*stop*) adjacent to the door opening with inner figure might be suggestive of the hidden father-daughter relationship.

Drawing 1

Drawing 1A. CAROL'S F-C-C-D: MOTHER-CENTERED

Notice the fewer symbols in Drawing 1A. The father and the star medallion are above. In real life, the mother was cold and very jealous of anyone taking her husband from her. She was jealous of her own daughter. The star as a symbol of emotional deprivation will be seen throughout our drawings.

Drawing 1A

Drawing 1B. CAROL'S F-C-C-D: SELF-CENTERED

Notice the sad expression on Carol's face and the stars between her son and self. Carol was divorced. She had difficulty nurturing her son. See how her dog is ascendant over the son. She loves her dog. See the "X" on the door to her house. The "X" as a symbol of ambivalence has been discussed by Burns (1972, 1982, 1987). The heavy roof atop the drawing is suggestive of a strong conscience. Burns (1987).

Carol's drawing of herself suggests a deprived child who is unable to mother adequately. We will have more to say about stars and deprivation and other F-C-C-D symbols.

Drawing 1B

PARENTS-SELF-CENTERED DRAWINGS

When one places the self and both parents in the center of a drawing and visually free associates around the periphery, a Parents-Self-Centered Circle Drawing (P-S-C-D) may be obtained.

Instructions for Obtaining a Parents-Self-Centered Drawing

The drawer is given a standard sheet of typing paper (8½ × 11 inches) with a circle drawn on the paper (7½ to 9 inch diameter). The instructions are: *"Draw your parents and yourself in the center of the circle. Visually free associate with drawn symbols around the periphery of the circle. Try to draw whole people, not stick or cartoon figures."*

Drawing 2. RONALD'S P-S-C-D: SEDUCTIVE MOTHER, HITLER COMPLEX

Ronald was a business executive, age 43, who had never been married. He was an only child beloved by a controlling mother married to a man some 20 years her senior. Ronald "never trusted women," had frequent anxiety attacks, and was chronically unhappy. Freudians would define Ronald's case as that of "an unresolved oedipal," that is, rivalry with the father for the mother's affection. Ronald displayed many characteristics seen in Hitler, whom he admired.

The naked, seductive mother seems to be in control of the pathetic puppet-like self. The father sits passively reading but watching so intensely that his eye "pops out." The gun above the father and the menacing knife pointing toward the mother are symbols that invite further exploration.

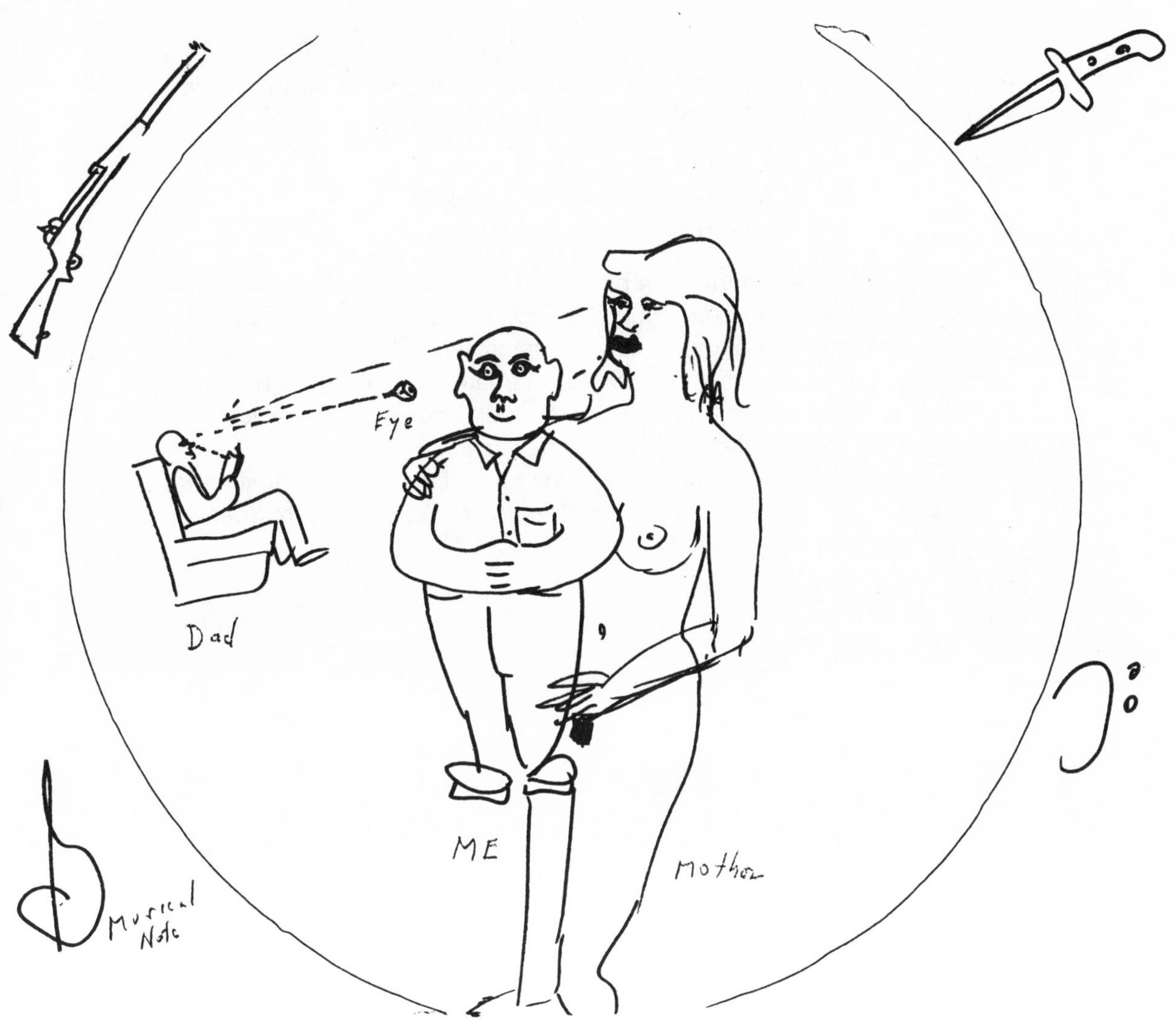

Drawing 2

SYMBOL-CENTERED PROBES

When one takes a symbol from the periphery of either an F-C-C-D or a P-S-C-D, centers this symbol, and visually free associates around the periphery, a Symbol-Centered Probe (SYM-C-P) may be obtained.

Instructions for Obtaining a Symbol-Centered Probe

The drawer may select the most positive or the most negative symbol from the periphery of the F-C-C-D or the P-S-C-D and center it in a SYM-C-P.

The drawer is given a standard sheet of typing paper ($8\frac{1}{2} \times 11$ inches) with a circle drawn on the paper ($7\frac{1}{2}$ to 9 inch diameter). The instructions for the SYM-C-P are: *"Center your chosen symbol and visually free associate with drawn symbols around the periphery of the circle."*

With younger or uneducated drawers, the instructions may be simplified to: *"Center your chosen symbol in the middle of the circle. Doodle whatever you want around the edge of the circle."*

Drawing 2A. RONALD'S SYMBOL-CENTERED PROBE (SYM-C-P): GUN-CENTERED

Directly above the gun is a symbol of execution. On the left the father is smashing the head of the self. The bullet from the gun, curiously similar to the eye in Drawing 2, passes through his head. The "dinosaur" mother adds to the violence of a world in which father destroys son—a chronic obsession with Ronald.

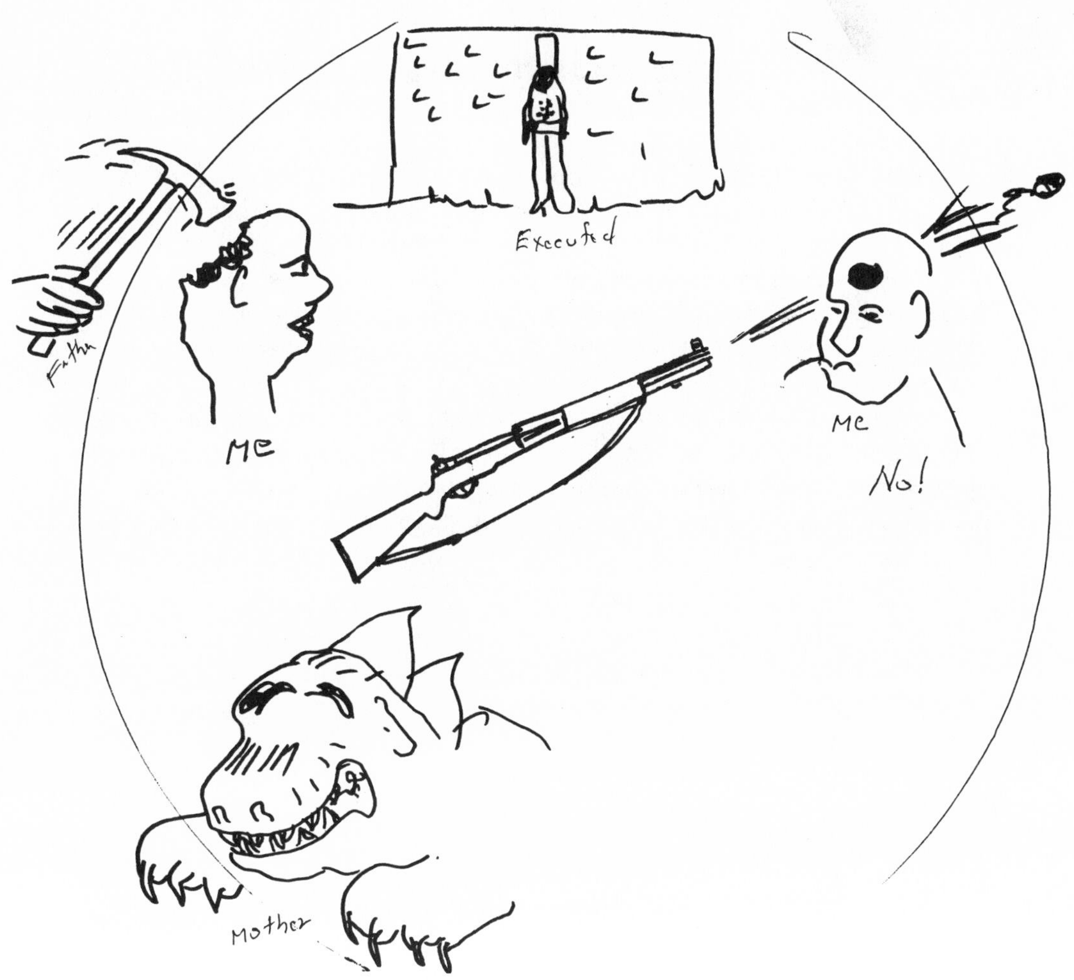
Executed
Father
Me
Me
No!
Mother

Drawing 2A

Drawing 2B. RONALD'S SYMBOL-CENTERED PROBE (SYM-C-P): KNIFE-CENTERED

Ronald drew his peripheral symbols counterclockwise. First is the cut-bread symbolic of Ronald's ever-present castration fears. Next comes the Hitler symbol representing "superman from the super race." Hitler is followed by the beckoning seductive mother saying "c'mon here."

Ronald's visual free association in Drawing 2B may be abbreviated to: castration fear—superman, counter phobic, anti-hero, accessible, seductive mother.

Ronald worked hard to understand himself and thus lower his stress level. He was not psychotic, as was Hitler. Through hard work in counseling, he gained control of himself. Ronald wasn't "cured" but he became more of a Woody Allen-like, chronically worried neurotic rather than a psychotic killer like Hitler.

Drawing 2B

Drawing 3. BOB'S P-S-C-D: ALCOHOLIC SON OF A REJECTING SISTER-MOTHER

Bob, a university senior, made Drawing 3. At the time he made his P-S-C-D, Bob was dropping out of the university, drinking heavily, and wanting to "go home." In making Drawing 3, Bob blocked in placing symbols around the circle, but kept trying. The symbols appeared outside the circle rather than inside.

It is important to allow the drawer to place the symbols where they choose, that is, inside the circle or outside. Drawers placing symbols outside the circle seem to have energy centers (condensed in symbols) farther from their center and thus more unconscious.

Bob described his mother as "hep." He felt she was more an aggressive sister than a mother. In the P-S-C-D, his mother is dressed in red (usually a child's color—Santa Claus in blue would not "feel right"). The self is closer to the father than to the mother. The mother's piercing eyes and "hard" face make her formidable.

On the mother's side of the P-S-C-D we see symbols in the top right which Bob describes as tension. At the bottom is a piercing eye and a "baby." The baby part of Bob seems to be waiting for the "hep" mother to see him and to meet his dependency needs. Repetition of human figures in a P-S-C-D frequently reflects "alter egos" or shadow people. Bob's baby seems a shadow or unconscious part of himself in control of his life at the time the drawing was made.

On the dad's side we see symbols of growth (flower), peace, and rocket power. Bob has a positive relationship to his father and stands close to him. The relation to the mother is grossly distorted. Bob's child is still struggling to receive love or acceptance from an immature mother. Look more carefully at the self and mother figures. See how the self and mother figures are "unbalanced." The self's shoulder adjacent to the mother is larger than the other and "moves" toward the mother's shoulder. The mother's shoulder adjacent to the son is enlarged. The father's shoulders are balanced.

The distortions on the self and mother suggest a desire by Bob for closeness. The baby is forcing Bob to quit school and return home, perhaps in hopes of receiving love from the maternal part of the "hep" mother. The crew-cut baby being watched seemed a likely symbol for further exploration.

(continued on page 18)

tension
anger
Dad
Self
MOM
peace
baby
"Hep" Mother
who is sister

Drawing 3

Just as a surgeon probes deeper to find the "cause" of a physical disturbance, a Symbol-Centered Probe may help us to go deeper toward the center to discover the "cause" of a psychological disturbance.

Drawing 3A. BOB'S SYMBOL-CENTERED PROBE (SYM-C-P): BABY-CENTERED

Bob was asked to place his P-S-C-D baby as the center in a SYM-C-P. As he drew the baby, Bob was unable to control its size and expressed "surprise" at how "big" the baby was.

The baby is surrounded by symbols associated by Bob with a "happy babyhood." Bob said he wanted to "quit school and go home and ride my bicycle for two years." The symbols in the SYM-C-P are all pleasant. The fierce-eyed baby was determined to be seen and to be babied.

In a dialogue with Bob, the fierce-eyed baby and the therapist reached a compromise. The baby wanted to quit school in the middle of the quarter and return home to another state. However, the compromise allowed Bob to finish the quarter and then return home to "help" the mother. The baby was fiercely determined to be seen by the mother. Bob's shadow baby was autonomous and powerful and very demanding. In one session utilizing drawing and symbol probes, Bob was able to get in touch with his very angry child. Lying on a couch talking about his "regressions" might have taken much longer. "One picture is worth ten thousand words."

block
Birthday cake for 1-year old
Football
"Father played football and I watched him when I was young"
smile
"like a baby looking up to see an adult smile"
Love
Bicycle
XMAS Tree presents
"chicken hat I had as a baby"

Drawing 3A

Chapter 2

FAMILY-CENTERED CIRCLE DRAWINGS (F-C-C-D)

VERBAL FREE ASSOCIATION

Talking therapy was made famous by Freud who analyzed words. His primary healing technique was verbal free association. The vast majority of psychotherapists in the western world follow Freud in attempting to heal through talking. People feel better after having shared their "feelings." Yet, feelings shared through words can often be shallow and distilled.

SIGN AND SYMBOL SYSTEMS IN HEALING

Language is limited to a sign system in which the coder and decoder are familiar with the words. Signs are abstract and have objective meanings. The goal of Freudian healing is to make the unconscious conscious through use of a free-associated sign system, i.e. words.

Healers like Carl Jung (1953, 1959, 1966, 1969) understood the limitations of sign systems and chose to focus on symbol systems. While signs (words) have objective meanings, symbols point to subjective feelings. Symbols may function as connecting links between levels of consciousness and be expressed in a great variety of cultural forms, including drawing, painting, sculptures, song, dance, ritual, movement, and architecture.

Freud tended to link dream symbols to sexual dynamics. Jung tended to link dream symbols to mythology, alchemy, and religious texts.

Symbols have universality not found in various language sign systems. Thus, it would be ideal for a healer to be aware of both sign and symbol systems. Sometimes a drawing becomes a "door-opener" allowing communication with parts of an individual not available through words.

VISUAL FREE ASSOCIATION IN THE F-C-C-D

Freud developed the technique of free association—chaining words together, moving from conscious to unconscious verbal material. In the Family-Centered-Circle Drawing (F-C-C-D) we chain visual symbols around a central family member.

For many people, the central point in their life is their father or mother. As a result, a technique of having the father, mother or self in the middle of a circle and having the person surround the central symbol with whatever comes to mind in visual free association is a valuable clinical tool: the Family-Centered Circle Drawing utilizing visual free association.

Some Things to Look for in an F-C-C-D

1. The relative size of figures, reflecting the psychological size of each and the energy invested in a figure.
2. The omission or overemphasis of parts of the body.
3. Facial expressions. Who is smiling or frowning, happy or sad? Do the figures have eyes—do they see?
4. The symbol directly above a figure. This symbol is often associated with primary feelings associated with this person. A heart directly above a figure may signify love; a knife above a figure suggests anger.
5. Are the symbols surrounding the self repeated in the parental drawings?
6. Is the self repeated in one or both of the parental drawings?
7. Which figures have buttons suggesting attachment?
8. Are the symbols surrounding the figures positive or negative?

These are a few of the things to look for; many more will become apparent.

Emily's F-C-C-Ds

IN LOVE WITH BRUCE SPRINGSTEEN; MOTHER IN LOVE WITH ELVIS PRESLEY

Drawing 4F. FATHER-CENTERED

Drawing 4F was done by 34-year-old Emily. Her father is placed in the center. Above him are swings. She mentions that her father promised that if she stopped sucking her thumb he would buy her a swing set, which he never did. On the top left is a boat. The father promised to take her boating, but didn't. The boat symbolizes the unfulfilled promises of her father and her lack of faith in him. The father had remarried and the stepmother is on the right. The stove symbolizes Emily's need to be nurtured by the father figure and the warmth associated with her fantasies of him. The shoes in the bottom left-hand corner are symbols of the need for stability.

This is a boat (really)
swing set
DADS WIFE
DAD
stove
running shoes
vacation

Drawing 4F

Drawing 4M. MOTHER-CENTERED

In Drawing 4M, Emily's mother is the central figure. At the top right of the F-C-C-D is a figure of Elvis Presley, with whom the mother had a fantasy romance. The TV symbolized for Emily the fantasy world in which her mother lived.

In the bottom right quadrant, Emily draws herself as sick and despondent, which in real life she often became in trying to get attention from the ungiving mother.

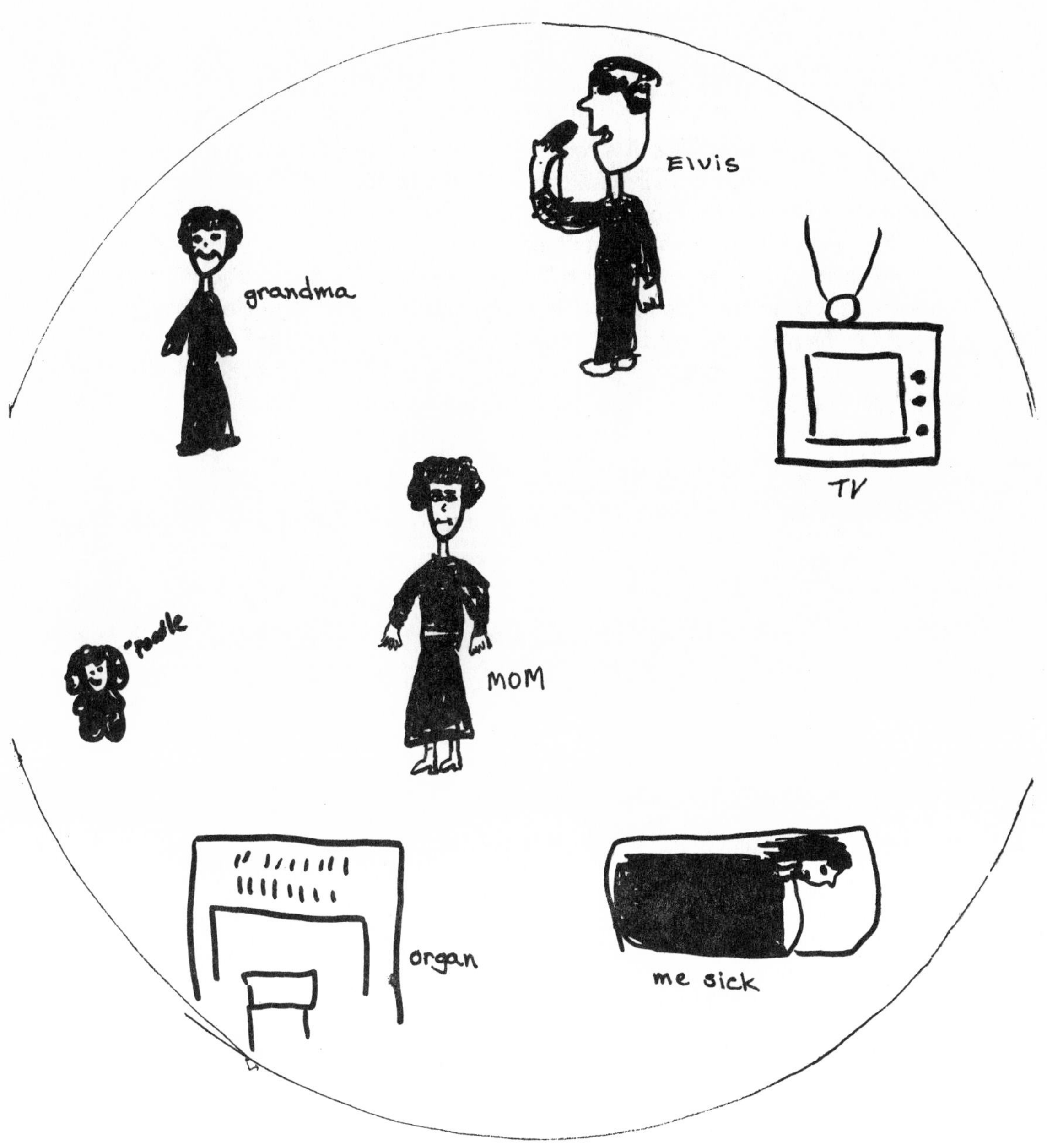

Drawing 4M

Drawing 4S. SELF-CENTERED

In Drawing 4S, Emily's self is centered. In the top right-hand corner we see Bruce Springsteen, whom Emily idolized. In the bottom right-hand quadrant we see Ted, with whom Emily lived. Ted was very nurturing and caring, but her fantasy relation to Bruce was much more powerful than her realistic relationship with Ted, just as her mother's relationship to Elvis Presley had been much more powerful than her relationship with her husband. The horse was a symbol which preoccupied Emily, as it does many girl-women fixated at a pubertal or "teeny-bopper" stage of development. The horse as a symbol in Kinetic Drawings has been discussed in detail (Burns, 1972).

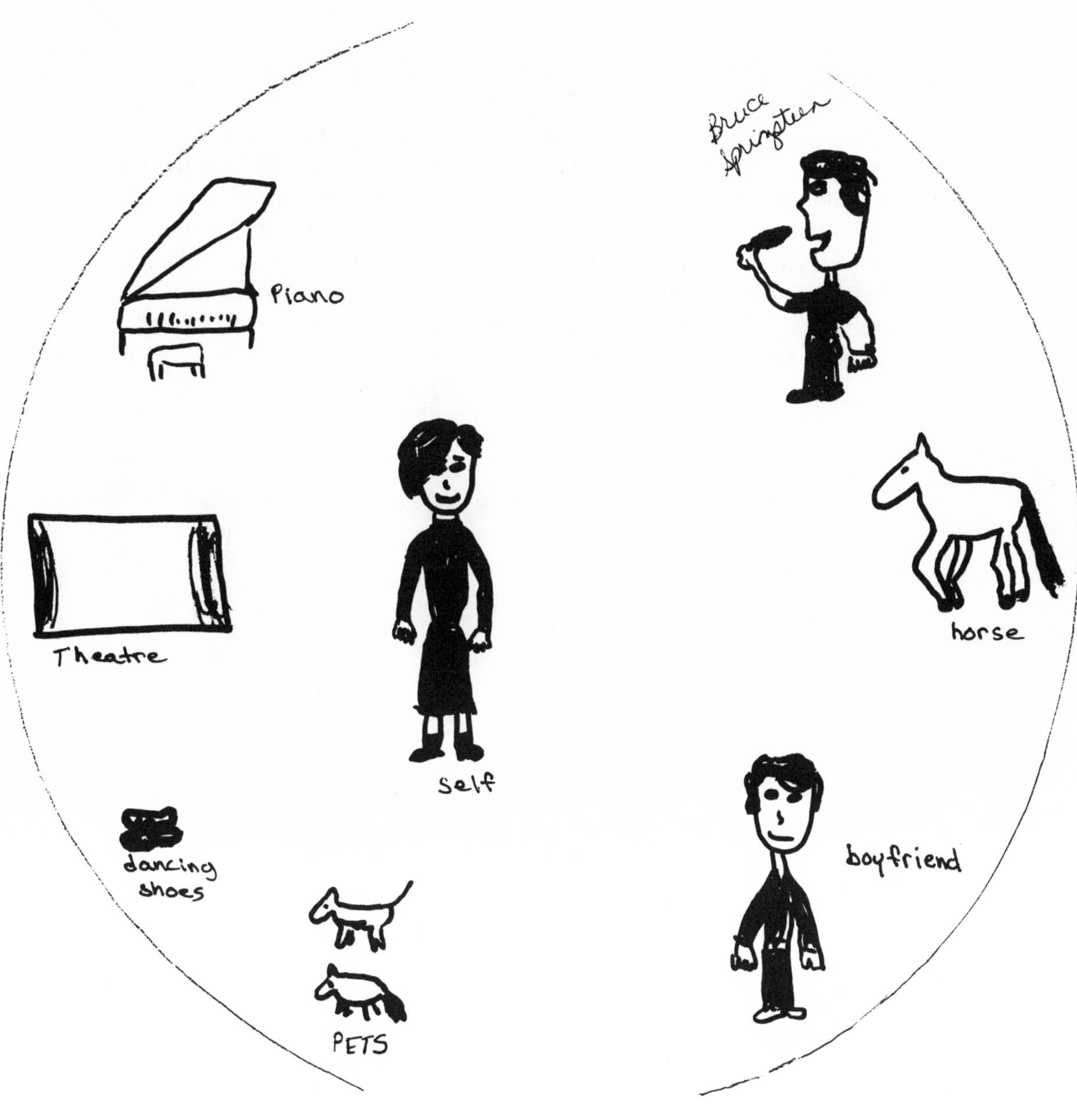
Bruce Springsteen
Piano
Theatre
self
horse
dancing shoes
PETS
boyfriend

Drawing 4S

Drawing 4C. COMPOSITE 4M and 4S

If we superimpose Emily's drawing 4S over Drawing 4M, we have a composite 3D-F-C-C-D. Bruce Springsteen and Elvis Presley are in the same part of circle and in identical positions. The boyfriend merges with the sickbed where he nurtures her in a motherly way. Emily's F-C-C-D and 3D-F-C-C-D gave us numerous insights useful in helping her. Emily's great crush on Bruce Springsteen was a repetition of her mother's crush on Elvis Presley. The tragedy of both their lives was that fantasy and illusion were "above" and dominant over real relationships.

grndma
(From 8-M)
Elvis
presley
(From 8-M)
Bruce
Springsteen
(From 8-S)
TV
Horse
(From 8-S)
Self
(From 8-S)
MOM
(From 8-M
Boy Friend
(From 8S)
organ
(From 8-M)
Self
(From 8M)

Drawing 4C

Jan's F-C-C-Ds

ALCOHOLIC MOTHER

Drawing 5M. MOTHER-CENTERED

Drawing 5M is by 46-year-old Jan. Jan's mother was an alcoholic who struggled with this problem throughout her adult life. The Christmas tree is part of a theme seen in people who are deprived and have unmet nurturing needs. The bottles on the right are self explanatory. The prone figure at the top portrays the mother when drunk. The self figure does not appear in this drawing.

mother
drunk
bottle
x-mAS Tree
mom
bottle
Frying Pan
daisy
tulip
flowers

Drawing 5M

Drawing 5F. FATHER-CENTERED

In Drawing 5F, Jan's father-centered drawing, the house is on top and of primary importance. The sunshine is at the bottom. Next to the sunshine is a rock. Jan had always wanted her father to be a dependable "rock." The father had emphasized money and material gains, as indicated by the dollar signs on the right. Jan puts herself in the picture, as do people who identify with a parent. She puts a tree, perhaps symbolic of her growth, in this area and the car as a symbol of power.

Drawing 5F

Drawing 5S. SELF-CENTERED

Drawing 5S shows Jan's F-C-C-D with self centered. She drew a man-like figure and then put a dress on the outside, indicating her sex role ambivalence. Her four children by two previous marriages are at top. She repeats the symbol of her father who has remarried. We see the dollar signs which were in the father drawing. Jan has worked, been self sufficient, and married men who were rich. The rock symbol, repeated in the bottom right-hand quadrant, is extremely important to Jan in reflecting the stability she wanted from her father and her husband. Thus, the self drawing has some of the symbols seen in the father-centered drawing, but none of the symbols seen in the mother-centered drawing. Count the number of symbols taken from the father-centered drawing (house, tree, $, car, rock, self). Now count the number of symbols in Jan's mother-centered drawing also present in Jan's self-centered drawing: none. Jan has identified with her father's world and rejected her mother's alcoholic world.

The power of the drawing to elicit symbols and subjective feelings may be seen in Jan's drawings. Jan had used the word "rock" numerous times in describing her father and her husband. She had hoped they would be rocks of stability for her, but they abandoned her. Little emotion seemed attached to the word "rock." However while drawing the symbol of the rock, Jan started to cry. The visual symbol rock created by Jan had elicited deeper feelings than the word "rock." Jan's created visual rock had a shape, size, color, texture, placement, etc. not possible with the word rock. Jan created the *drawn* rock from within. The *word* "rock" had been created by someone else.

Drawing 5S

Nancy's F-C-C-Ds

ALCOHOLIC AND HYPOCHONDRIACAL MOTHER

Drawing 6M. MOTHER-CENTERED

Nancy was an only child, age 31. Her mother was an untreated alcoholic, reflected in the bottle-glass symbol. The mother was hypochondriacal and demanding.

Facial expressions in drawings are one of the more important features. Note the intense eyes of the mother and the evil feelings suggested by the face. This mother had only to call on the telephone to control Nancy and create great fear in her. The rosebush was the last drawn of the symbols. In many drawings, flowers are put in to help bring cheer to the picture and the centered figure.

The "ace" symbol conveyed Nancy's feeling that the mother always won.

Drawing 6M

Drawing 6F. FATHER-CENTERED

What does the father's expression convey? The blank expression and non-seeing eyes suggest a person very difficult to "know." Notice how Nancy places her self in this drawing, being pulled by the father. She does not appear in the mother drawing. Most of the symbols are related to traveling. Notice the large sun above the father, warming the picture. There is no sun in the mother drawing. As a child, Nancy was offered the choice of living in either the mother's world or the father's world. She chose the father's space.

ocean
Ship
Father
palm tree
globe
Father
Book
STRONG PERSONALITY
speed boat
me water Skiing

Drawing 6F

Drawing 6S. SELF-CENTERED

Note Nancy's relatively pleasant expression. Her small sun surrounded by clouds and an airplane suggests that Nancy does not expect much warmth. The passport and suitcase repeat the dominant travel motif seen in the father drawing. None of the symbols from the mother drawing are repeated in the self drawing. Nancy appears to have identified with the father's world. There are no bodies on the parental or self figures. Nancy tends to deny her feminine qualities, including her sexuality. She has many friends, but no one to love deeply. She places "a man" in her drawing who has the unseeing eyes of the father. She has internalized much of her father and the feminine part of her is incomplete and unfulfilled.

suitcase
Self
A man
Different people
Children
child-like experiences

Drawing 6S

Jeff's F-C-C-Ds

TEENAGE SON ATTACHED TO MOTHER

Drawing 7F. FATHER-CENTERED

Jeff, who made drawing 7F, was 18 at the time of the drawing and going to prison for auto theft. He had never felt close to his father. The TV news at the top of the drawing probably reflects the father's interest in the political power arena. The toucan was associated with the father's bird "hobby." He collected all kinds of pictures and statues of toucans, probably related to his desire to "fly away." The father frankly admitted he would like a new family with a son who would become an important political figure. The object at the bottom was a gadget the father manufactured. The pot of "good food" symbolizes Jeff's dream to be nurtured by an ambitious non-nurturing father who admitted he couldn't feel "love," only ambition.

NEWS
Toucan
bird makes
lot of noise
throws food
around
Pot full of
Good Food
DAD

Drawing 7F

Drawing 7M. MOTHER-CENTERED

Jeff's mother, seen in Drawing 7M, had tried to be both father and mother in the family. In drawing the family, Jeff put color into the mother, but not into any other family member. The symbols of food, family, flowers, and friends all are positive feelings toward mom. The buttons on the mom reflect Jeff's attachment to her. Jeff fought against this attachment by being macho on the outside to compensate for his closeness to Mom on the inside.

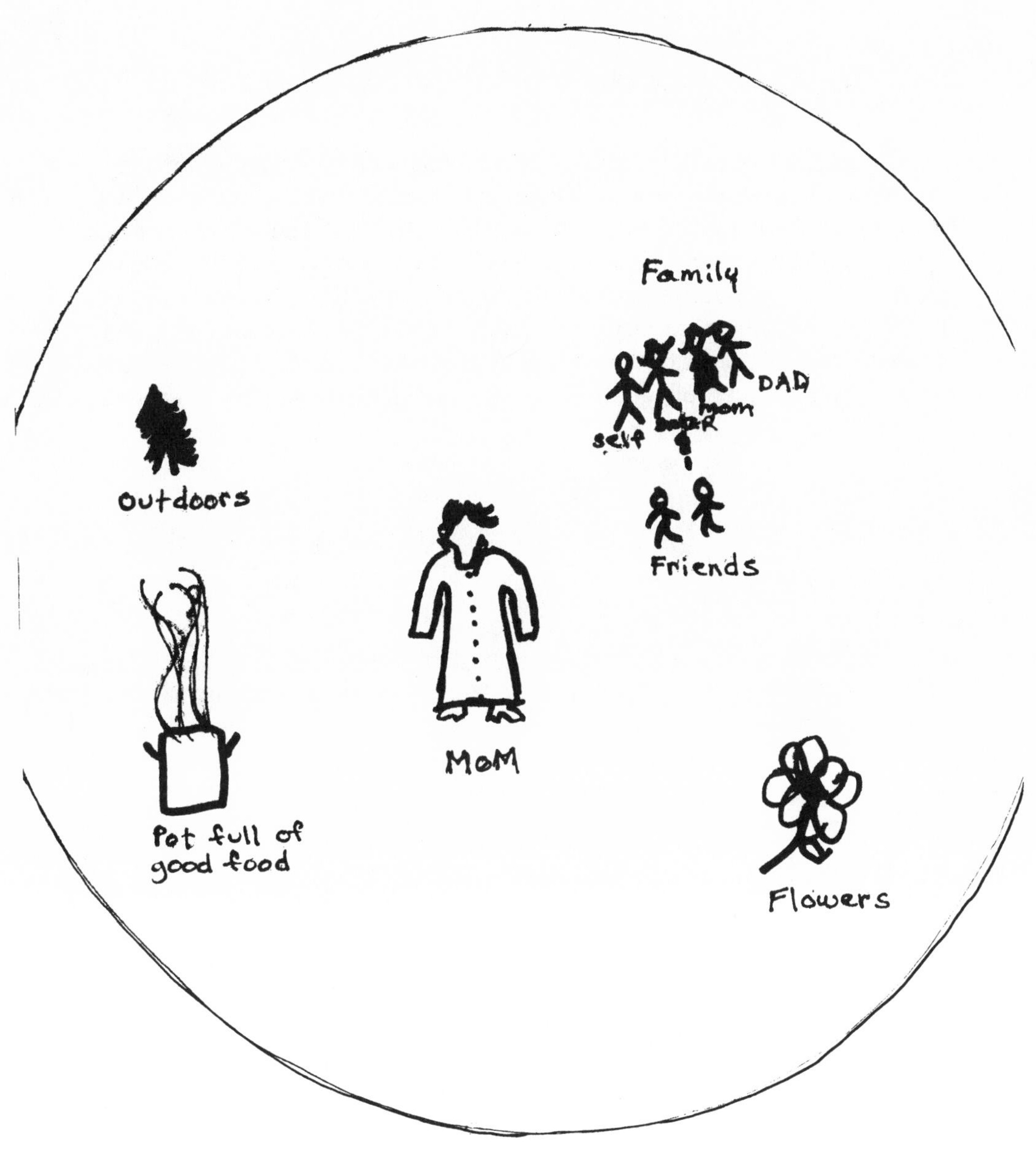
Family
DAD
mom
self
outdoors
Friends
MoM
Pot full of
good food
Flowers

Drawing 7M

Drawing 7S. SELF-CENTERED

Jeff's self drawing shows none of the symbols seen in the father drawing. The tree and the people are symbols repeated from the mother drawing. If we superimpose the drawings, we see that Jeff has substituted "party" for "pot full of good food" and indeed Jeff had "partied" rather than gone to school. Jeff's "girl" is seen in the quadrant where mother has family and friends and father has a bird. Jeff's love of money and cars seems part of his compensation for his inability to get power through identification with Dad. Although 18 years old and over six feet tall, Jeff's self-image is much smaller than Mother's or Father's.

Drawing 7S

Mary's F-C-C-Ds

WOMAN'S EMERGENCE

Drawing 8M. MOTHER-CENTERED

Forty-seven-year-old Mary surrounded her mother with unpleasant symbols. Her mother has been a martyr. In her mother drawing, Mary places the hospital bed in the top corner; her mother was chronically ill with vague symptoms. The lonely boat on the water reflects the depressive mood in the mother's brown world. The drudgery of kitchen work and the sink and stove suggest a colorless world of work. The "colorful" grandma at the bottom was added last to give the drawing some color and perhaps help the mother.

Drawing 8M

Drawing 8F. FATHER-CENTERED

Father's world is essentially black, a reflection of his usually black mood. His special chair where he sat and often pontificated is black. However, Mary tries to brighten his world with her red color and even a red picture of herself on father's black desk. Despite his black moods, Mary preferred his world to that of the martyr mother. Father was intelligent, well informed, and very religious. Mary places two images of herself in father's world. Her self in this world is larger than the father and much larger than the mother. In drawing 8F, Mary sees herself as larger and is the adult or parent to the parents. She still has attachment (buttons) to her father. Mary, however, is self-contained (buttons on herself); she had to meet her own needs in growing up. The church, the ascendant symbol in the father's world, became extremely important to Mary in her own development.

CHURCH
CAR
CHAIR
NEWSPAPER
SELF
PICTURE OF M.
DESK

Drawing 8F

Drawing 8S. SELF-CENTERED

Mary's self drawing is much more colorful than her mother and father drawings. The heart as a symbol of love is repeated as the central ascendant symbol. She has a patient, loving husband and three children. The buttons on the husband suggest her attachment to him. He touches her and smiles in contrast to the dour look of her father. Religion is still central for Mary. If we superimpose the father drawing over the self drawing, we see the heart-shaped figure behind the black, pointed, severe church of the father. Mary has substituted a gentle eastern religion for the harsh fundamentalist religion of the father. She is a therapist and has always derived a great deal of sunshine from the transactions with her clients. Her children are beneath the clients. She has a special relationship to her youngest daughter, who reaches out for her.

Through the insights obtained from free association to the visual symbols of the F-C-C-Ds, Mary continued her self-growth process. She had been a "talking" therapist for many years and has experienced talking therapy for herself. When she incorporated visual techniques, including visual free association, with her talking, Mary changed and improved dramatically. Her own children were surprised at her transformation.

BALLET
SLIPPERS
CLIENT
CLIENT
HUSBAND
TRANS
FOR
MA
TION
SELF
CHILDREN

Drawing 8S

Paul's F-C-C-Ds

ACADEMIC INVALID

Paul at the time of these drawings was 25 years old, but socially closer to 13. He was indecisive about work and school. He had a long history of difficulties in school and "learning disorders." He came from a large family with parents who had been devoutly religious but who had changed in the last year. Paul was in a state of transformation, as was the entire family.

Drawing 9F. FATHER-CENTERED

The father is solid-appearing with buttons. Paul repeats himself twice in this drawing, both times as a little boy playing games with Dad. The central church symbol above Dad suggests Paul's interest in this area associated with the father. The father was a creative person trapped at a "desk" job and Paul captures this image beneath the father's feet. The 13 trees enclosed in the mountain with "the kids playing" suggest Paul's fixation at about a 13-year-old level.

Drawing 9F

Drawing 9M. MOTHER-CENTERED

The broad-shouldered, stern-appearing mother centers Paul's mother drawing. He places himself in two places in the drawing. One self is bedridden, with the mother comforting him. This role was one Paul played frequently with his mother. He was an underachiever, which brought the mother to his side. The other self figure is being lectured to by the mother. Conforming to mother's lectures brought him some conditional love. The home was important to Paul and is placed top and center in the picture. At age 25, he had just moved from home. The buttons on mother suggest his attachment to her.

Drawing 9M

Drawing 9S. SELF-CENTERED

In Paul's self drawing, we see how small the self is compared to the figures of the father and mother in his other drawings. Paul had just moved into a house with three female roommates and had a brother-sister relationship with them. He tended to displace his mother-attachment to the roommates, especially the one portrayed with buttons. Paul had some minimal success in sports and this success was important to him. Music also was a positive aspect of his life.

Paul's F-C-C-Ds helped him to understand his family attachments which kept him from growing. At age 25, he was growing up, got a job, moved to an apartment, bought a car, grew up socially, sexually, and financially, and was taking charge of his own transformation.

Roomates
basketball
athletic
Peace - water plant
nature
SELF
music

Drawing 9S

Dora's F-C-C-Ds

OVERWEIGHT WITH REJECTION OF MOTHER

Dora, 37 years old, had a chronic problem of overweight. She had been sent to "fat farms" since prepuberty. Her father was a workaholic and her mother a subservient, unfulfilled woman. Dora was the youngest of four children. She has been married some 15 years and has a daughter.

Drawing 10M. MOTHER-CENTERED

There are several symbols surrounding the mother suggesting her depressive tendencies, for example, the teardrops on the left and the black cloud on the right. The rug suggests her mother's "walked upon" quality. The cookie on the right and the cookie jar characterized as "stingy" suggest Dora's difficulty in having oral needs met by her mother. Mother had big cars and jewelry as slight compensation for her lonely life married to a workaholic. The vibrant red heart at the bottom seems a pathetic attempt to brighten her mother's life.

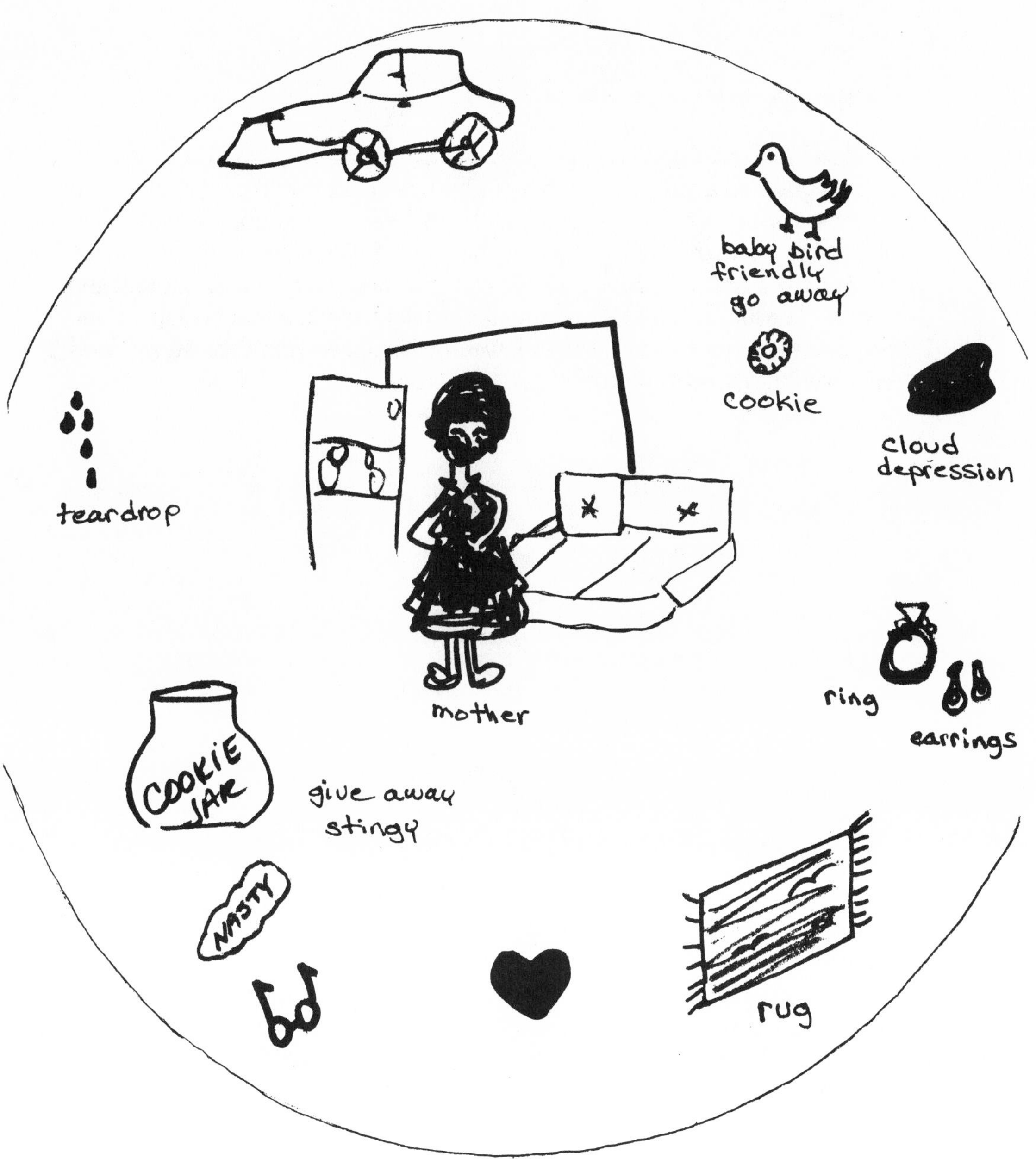
baby bird
friendly
go away
cookie
cloud
depression
teardrop
mother
ring
earrings
COOKIE
JAR
give away
stingy
NASTY
rug

Drawing 10M

Drawing 10F. FATHER-CENTERED

Dora fills the father drawing with symbols of success—big house, big car, dollar signs, and a golf course where father spent much of his spare time with business associates. The smiles on the right were symbolic of a certain phoniness in father's smiles. The huge hands and shoulders reflect Dora's awe of his power, also associated with the "mean and nasty" description at the bottom. The tall, powerful tree characterized her feelings about her father. She saw herself as a tiny tree, overshadowed by her father and thus stunted and frustrated in her own growth.

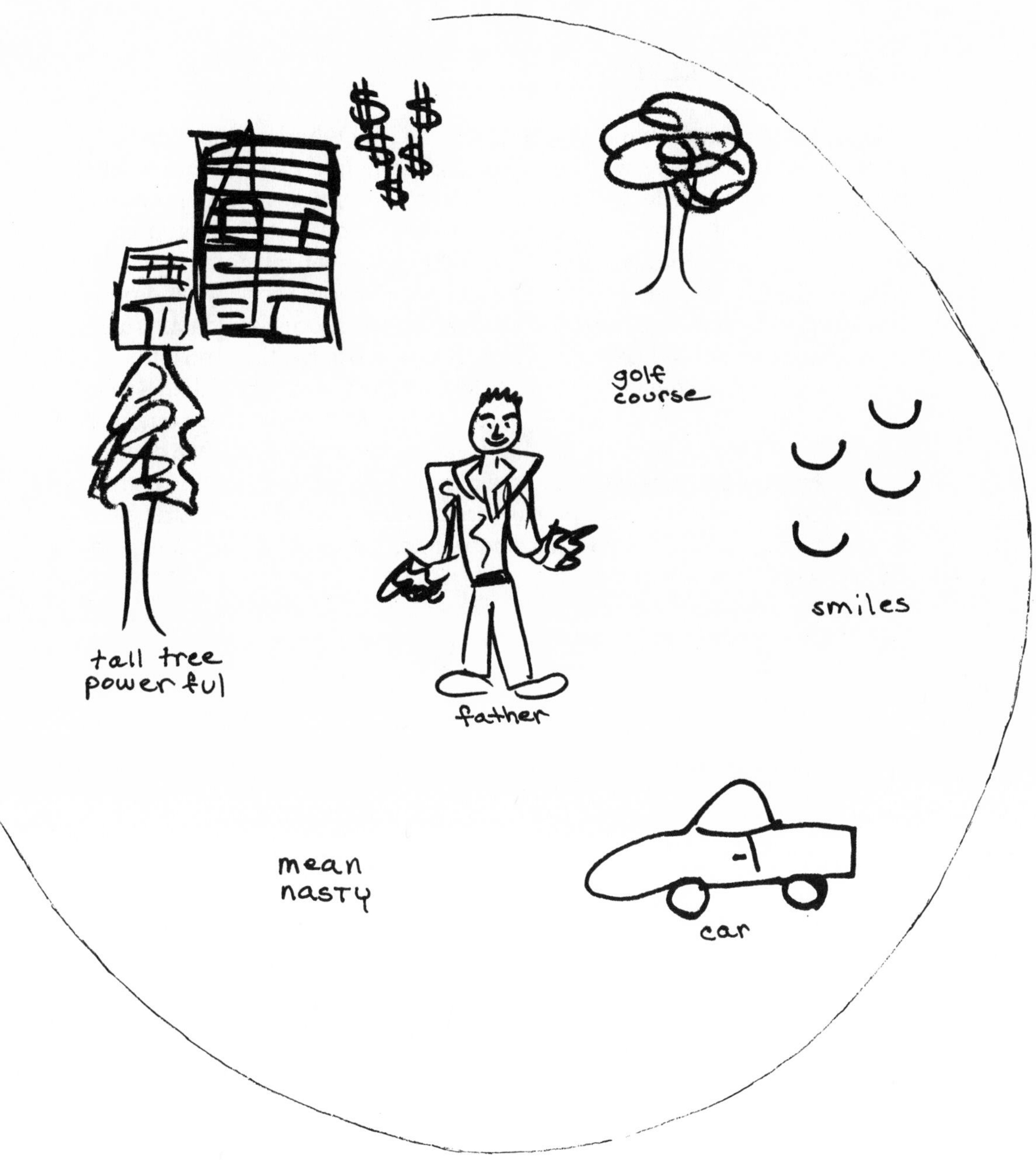
golf
course
smiles
tall tree
powerful
father
mean
nasty
car

Drawing 10F

Drawing 10S. SELF-CENTERED

If we cut out the central figures in Dora's F-C-C-Ds and set them up as a paper family, the sizes suggest that Dora viewed herself as a little girl, which psychologically was true. Drawing 10S has some of the symbols from the father drawing—the phony smiles and the "mean and nasty." The top symbols in the father and mother drawings reflect power—car and dollar sign. The top symbol in Dora's self drawing is a table where people socialize and play. Dora has not incorporated the parent's emphasis on success and money and jewelry. She remains a child-mother. Her relationship to her husband is that of a sister who is often "mean and nasty." Her relationship to her children is that of a sister often "mean and nasty." Dora is fixated at a younger age and has rejected both parental models. She has fallen in love with herself. At a deeper level, Dora would not compete with the mother. She felt sorry for the mother and so remains little and uncompetitive in all areas of her life. Dora struggled hard in therapy and changed considerably after the death of her father, the mighty overshadowing tree symbol.

no stress
socialize
play
my job as mother
childish
my book
Job
Place eat feed people
daughters
self
smiles
stove
mean
nasty

Drawing 10S

Dan's F-C-C-Ds

SUCCESSFUL MAN STRUGGLING TO ACCEPT WOMEN

Dan is an exceptionally successful, unmarried business executive. Because of his father's health problems, it was necessary for Dan to start working at an early age. He has worked hard ever since and supported his parents in a luxurious style. At age 39, Dan was still trying to work out harmonious and loving relationships with women.

Drawing 11F. FATHER-CENTERED

Dan's father figure is small and mild appearing, surrounded simply by house, car, and fire to warm him. The "close-up of father" in the bottom right-hand quadrant is different. Frequently in our family drawings we will see a self figure placed in the drawing of one of the parents. One suspects that the drawing of the "close-up of father" is a self portrait, that is, Dan was a father to his father by taking care of him financially and emotionally.

Drawing 11F

Drawing 11M. MOTHER-CENTERED

In contrast to Dan's mild looking father figure, the broad-shouldered mother appears grim and ominous. The "phony" smiles appear on the right as they did in drawing 10F. The nurturing symbols surrounding the mother are in contrast to the grim, purse-clutching, domineering mother. Dan tried hard to please and brighten his mother's life, but underneath this facade was a deep distrust and fear of her reflected in her face and broad shoulders. Dan's ambivalence toward the mother generalized to other women.

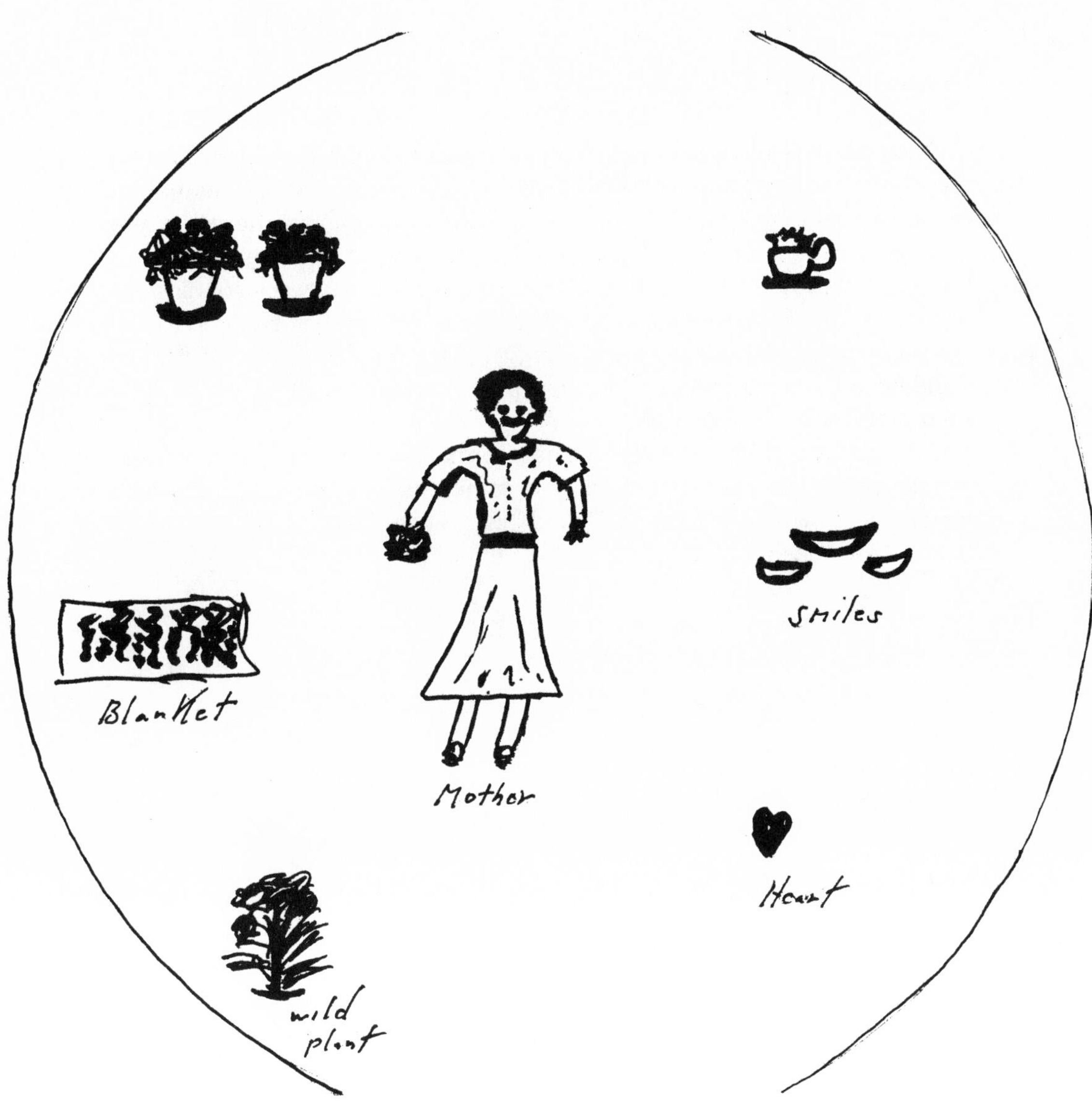

Drawing 11M

Drawing 11S. SELF-CENTERED

Dan's self drawing depicts a weak figure similar to that of the father. If we cut out the central figures in his F-C-C-Ds and make them a family, the mother would be the grim "boss." There is no symbol directly above the father and mother figures. Above his self figure Dan places a heart, perhaps symbolic of his search for love. To the right is a stream with rocks suggestive of his tears and depression in seeking love from the "rock-like" mother. He tried to feel loved by having many friends and "hugging" people. He gained respect by standing on a podium lecturing. Dan puts emphasis on his own growth, suggested by the tree symbol.

Dan made great strides in his own transformation and slowly accepted and trusted women at a deeper level. The family drawing provided him with insights and symbols which facilitated his growth. Dan has been happily married for one-and-a-half years and continues to grow.

stream with rocks
Self
Podium
self: hugging people

Drawing 11S

Howard's F-C-C-Ds

A REFORMED ALCOHOLIC DEPENDENT UPON HIS WIFE FOR SURVIVAL

Howard is 47 and a successful businessman. He was an alcoholic until about six years ago. With help and support from his wife, he has stayed "on the wagon." Howard is unsure of himself and his wife makes most of the family decisions.

Drawing 12M. MOTHER-CENTERED

Howard's rather woebegone-appearing mother is surrounded by three symbols. The top barred window is described as the mother's obsession with physical controls. The numerous houses suggest his nomadic existence associated with his feelings of having been uprooted. The presents suggest Howard's gifts to his depressed mother.

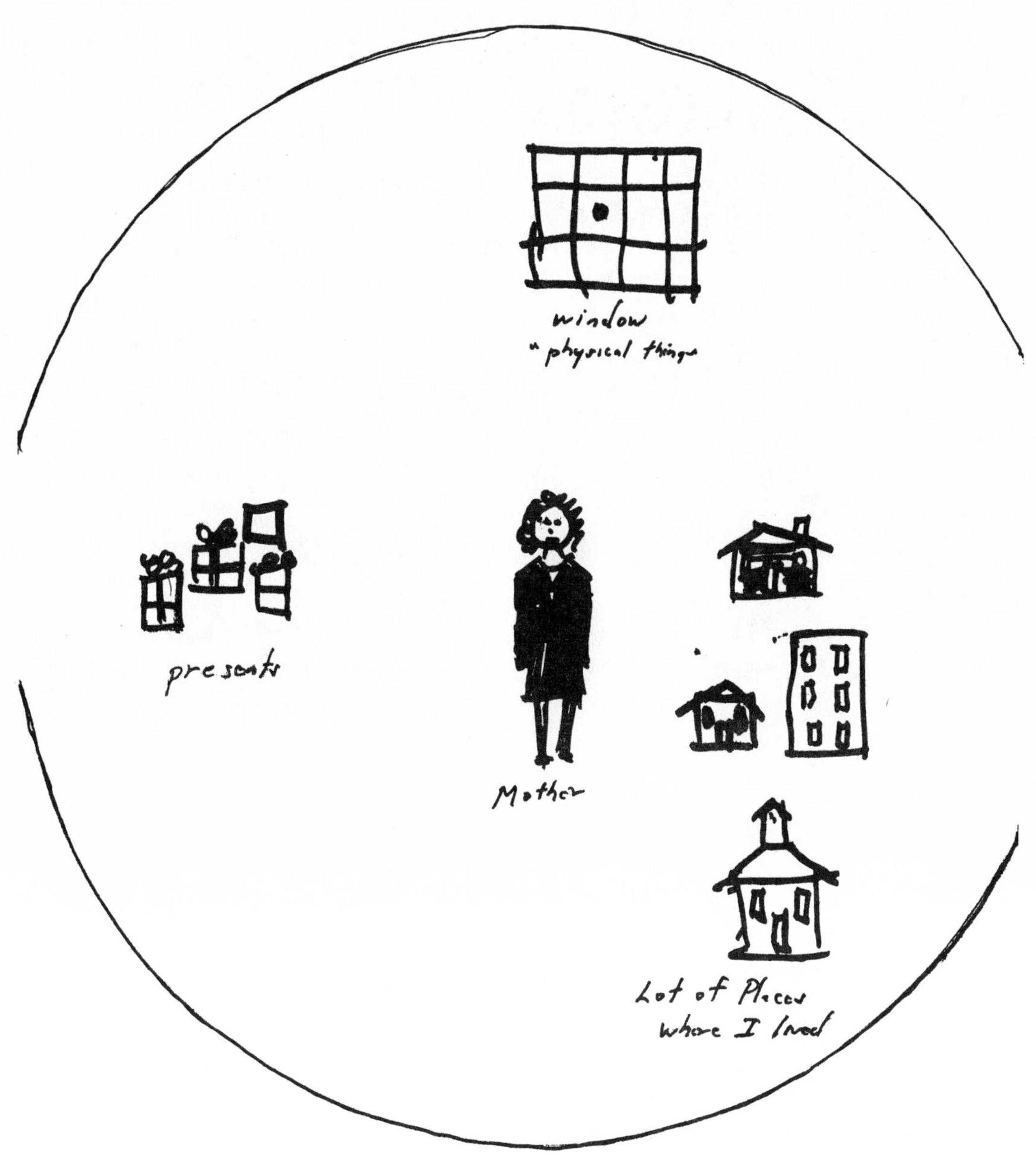
window
= physical things
presents
Mother
Lot of Places
where I lived

Drawing 12M

Drawing 12F. FATHER-CENTERED

Howard places himself in the father drawing, showing his preference for the father. The bible symbol is directly above the father's head. The dog in the top of the drawing reflects his perception of the father's passive role. The "something bright" was added last as if to cheer up the rather blue drawing.

Dog
Bible
Bird
something bright
step-Mother
step-sister
Father
self
Mobile Home

Drawing 12F

Drawing 12S. SELF-CENTERED

The dog and cat figures are placed directly above the self. For Howard, the cat symbolizes his wife and the subservient dog symbolizes himself. The colorful wife brightens the otherwise brown-grey-blue drawing. The wife faces the grandson whom she enjoys nurturing. Howard enjoys being nurtured, too. At a deeper level, he resented his dependency upon his wife and his ambivalence toward her was the focal point in his therapy.

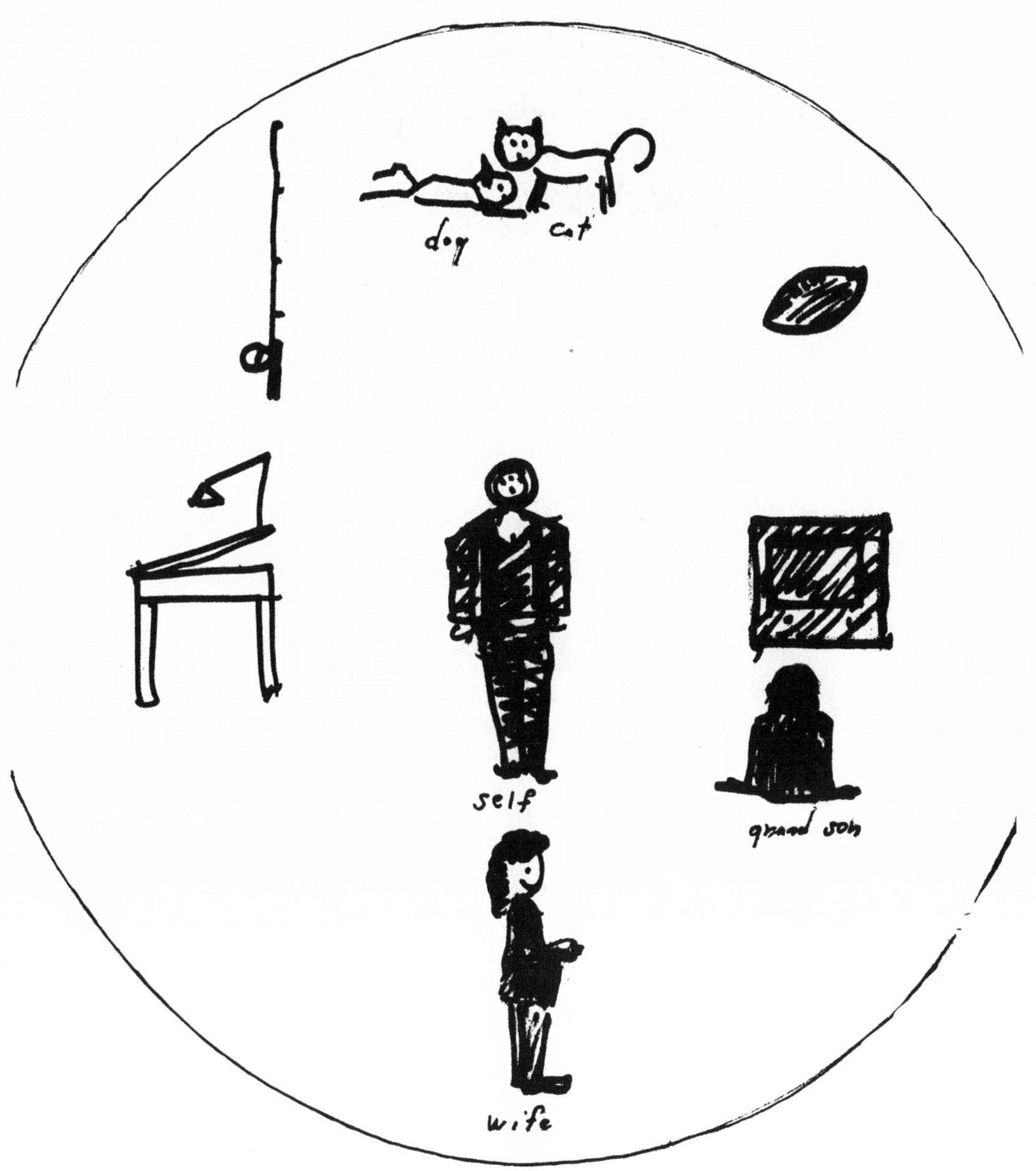

Drawing 12S

Jane's F-C-C-Ds

ALCOHOLIC FATHER

Drawing 13F. FATHER-CENTERED

Drawing 13F is 31-year-old Jane's father drawing. The bottles surround him reflecting his alcoholism and the "lies" indicates her distrust of him. The father is encapsulated, a technique used in a drawing to isolate an unwanted energy.

Drawing 13F

Drawing 13M. MOTHER-CENTERED

Drawing 13M shows the mother next to her two sons, her favorites. There is a house at the top with two trees growing. These two trees may symbolize the two sons who were the "apples of the mother's eyes." The mother was also a member of a tennis club and was gone a lot. In comparing drawing 13F and 13M, one can see more color and positive aspects in the mother drawing.

Drawing 13M

Drawing 13S. SELF-CENTERED

In drawing 13S, Jane is close to her six-year-old son and to her husband. We see her home at the top with the sun radiating all around, permeating the lives of everybody in her family. Jane has worked out her problems after having married a man who had problems similar to her father's. She succeeded in helping him get straightened out and enjoy his home and family life. This is a very determined young woman who has worked out her problems realistically, who enjoys her family, and is intensely involved in her own growth and development. Jane has identified with neither of her parents, but has become self-sufficient. Notice how the self figure in this drawing is much larger than the father or the mother in drawing 13M and 13F. This suggests the self has outgrown her parents.

Drawing 13S

Tina's F-C-C-Ds

CONTROLLING, NON-NURTURING MOTHER

Drawing 14F. FATHER-CENTERED

The prone father being "henpecked" by his wife is clearly depicted in drawing 14F. The relatively impoverished world of the "couch potato" father is not one most of us would like. His ascendant car appears most important to him from Tina's view.

Drawing 14F

Drawing 14M. MOTHER-CENTERED

The "hard" expression of the controlling mother in drawing 14M symbolizes Tina's feelings about her mother. She is afraid of her judgmental mother. The mother loves "sales," as seen by the symbol above her head. She buys old clothes to fix up for the family. The hangers above the mother's head are frequently reflective of "hooks" in the mind of the drawer. Tina has severe headaches when drawn into the mother's world. The mother is often manic and clutters the house with her collections. Tina has many unresolved conflicts with this controlling, judgmental mother.

Drawing 14M

Drawing 14S. SELF-CENTERED

Tina is happily married and has successfully raised three children. Her self drawing depicts a world most of us would like to live in. With her family and friends, her world is idyllic. But when the phone rang and her mother called, she became very disturbed and had "headaches."

Tina worked hard to resolve her relation to her parents. Her father's perceived weakness and her mother's "bossiness" were finally accepted. She would visit their world with forgiveness and understanding. The "hooks" from the mother were removed and Tina's headaches were alleviated.

OFFICE
TOOTHPASTE
Self
Husband
children
BANK STATEMENT
Tennis Friends
Self

Drawing 14S

Cherie's F-C-C-Ds

WOMAN MARRYING ALCOHOLIC MEN SIMILAR TO HER FATHER

Drawing 15F. FATHER-CENTERED

Cherie's father was a minister and an alcoholic. He sexually molested two of his daughters and some of his parishioners. He was unable to nurture his three children at the bottom of the F-C-C-D. At the top we see symbols most important to him—his collection of old records, his church books, and fishing rods and guns related to his outdoor activities. See how the parishioners are larger, more colorful, and more ascendant than his children.

Father holds a drink in one hand and a cigarette and a book in the other. Books held at the midline are frequently feminine sexual symbols (Burns, 1982). Father is colored black and his face is grim. His crotch is "scalloped," typical of drawers avoiding the sexual area.

The pathetic, pink self figure appears a grossly neglected and pathetic baby—but a tenacious baby. Cherie never gave up in her pathetic, unconscious attempt to have her father love and nurture her.

stereo - music
church
books
parishioners
office people
cigarette
Book
fishingrods
car
guns
Father
typewriter
children
Self

Drawing 15F

Drawing 15M. MOTHER-CENTERED

Cherie's mother all dressed in red holds her drink and cigarette and is depicted as a hostess. Cherie does not place herself in this drawing. Her mother was not interested in her children. Notice the small size of the mother, who was a sister to her own children and unable to nurture them. She is surrounded by her friends and bottles. The telephone and tennis racket and balls reflect the long hours on the phone talking to friends and her tennis games with friends. The TV also took her away from her family. Music was her solace and she fled to her piano when sad.

Cherie's mother was overwhelmed with the father's acting-out sexual behavior. Her drinking seemed a way to escape from him. Unfortunately, she also withdrew from her children.

PIANO
friends
cigarette
friend
Drink
Mother
(Hostess)
friends
TV

Drawing 15M

Drawing 15S. SELF-CENTERED

See how large Cherie's self is compared to the mother. She plays tennis and golf and has friends. She has taken the best from mother's world and improved upon it. She is surrounded by loved family including her nine-month-old daughter and four-year-old son. All are smiling. She loves her home and garden. Cherie depicts an ideal world for herself. Yet she is unhappy and searching. Tom is her third husband. All her husbands were alcoholics at the time of her marriages. They were all bright, "successful," rich, and had "high sex drives." At the time of this drawing, Cherie was divorcing her husband, Tom, who had been sober for five years, and was "going back" to her second husband who needed her and was drinking again.

Cherie's adult as depicted in her self F-C-C-D seemed unable to control her life. It was as if the pathetic little child depicted in her father drawing was "in charge." This pathetic child was tenacious—she was still looking for her father although he was dead. Cherie's little girl had control. She was looking for a father substitute—a man who drank too much, was bright and successful and sexy, and had all the qualities Cherie remembered about her father.

Why was she so obsessed with gaining father's love? If we go back to Drawing 15F, we see the father and the tiny deprived "babies" at the bottom. If we go back to 15M with the mother centered we see no family members. Mother gave nothing to her children but, being egocentric, took from them. The tiny crumbs of affection came only from the depressed, depraved, alcoholic father, but this affection seemed better than nothing and was desperately sought—even after father had died.

In counseling with Cherie, it helped to review her father's world as shown in Drawing 15F. Cherie had his record collection and listened to "his music" for long periods of time. She read books by authors he admired. She went hunting and fishing in places her father had been.

Cherie learned to see her obsessive attachments to her father in the symbols surrounding him in Drawing 15F. Each time she repeated activities associated with him, she was drawn into a world controlled by her pathetic, starved-for-love child-baby.

To help her healing process, these addictions were discontinued for a six-month period. No father symbols—records, authors, hunting, fishing, chasing father substitutes—were activated. Cherie stayed in her own "adult

(continued on page 96)

garden
House
car
friends
dogs
son 18
Self
Daughter
(9 months)
Step Daughter
(15
Husband
son
(8)
golf
clubs

Drawing 15S

center." She made friends with the pathetic child and invited her into her own space. The pathetic, addicted child and the fulfilled, happy adult became one.

Cherie decided to stay with husband, Tom. Tom, too, was told about the pathetic child and "adopted" her. When Cherie became sad and the waves of depression attached to the "poor baby" swept over her, both she and Tom comforted and nurtured this neglected child.

Two years later, Cherie and Tom are happy and growing. Cherie is centered and at peace with her past. She no longer searches for Dad outside. Cherie is centered and balanced and growing.

Rebecca's F-C-C-Ds

WOMAN'S UNCONSCIOUS SEARCH FOR UNGIVING, CHILDISH, WORKAHOLIC FATHER

Drawing 16F. FATHER-CENTERED

Father's eyes do not see. He was a workaholic—successful in his California business. At home he was a little boy who demanded to be pampered and the center of attention. The closed door suggests his daughter was never able to get inside his world. His argumentative nature is symbolized by the "blaring" mouths. The curious "Mickey Mouse" at the top of the drawing was interpreted by Rebecca as the phony, Disneyland relationship she had to this closed man. He was interested in sports; Rebecca became fascinated by sports. He was interested in buses; Rebecca was fascinated by buses. The heart at the bottom was drawn by Rebecca in an attempt to bring love to her father's space; Rebecca often brought love but did not receive love from this unseeing father living in his phony Mickey Mouse world.

Mickey
Mouse
Disneyland
Football
BASKETBALL
closed door
love
XX
XY
Father
Blaring
mouths
for agrivations
given
forth

Drawing 16F

Drawing 16M. MOTHER-CENTERED

Mother's eyes see. Her religion and love for her children are ascendant in the drawing. Yet there is a phoniness in the fixed, detached "happy smiling person" on the left. The frown symbolizes "the sense of sadness never really revealed until ill." Rebecca's mother died of cancer some five years prior to Drawing 16M. The mother had swallowed her angers and disappointments in living with such an ungiving, unseeing man. When desperately ill, she poured out all this anger to her daughter, who then realized how sad a married life her mother endured. Yet Rebecca appreciated her mother's attempts to love her and her sense of fair play.

synagogue
lots of Love to give to us kids
Happy smiling person
Scales of Balance
sense of fairplay
frown
sense of sadness
ear
always willing to listen to us kids
Mother

Drawing 16M

Drawing 16S. SELF-CENTERED

Rebecca looks like her mother in Drawing 16M. The heart, her husband, and her music are atop her drawing. She is surrounded by flowers and her sister's family. Rebecca was married and in love with her husband, who loved her. They had two children. Rebecca was loved by most everyone. She had a sense of fair play and people came to her for judgments and for someone willing to listen—characteristics she had given her mother in Drawing 16M.

The bottom parts of the drawing reflect a sadness in Rebecca. She feels "pulled in two directions—trying to change" like "trying to turn the page" in a book.

Rebecca was trying to be an adult but was pulled back to childhood. In her childhood she had pretended a lot. She pretended she was a princess and her father a king—a king who cared for her. In this Mickey Mouse pretend world, Rebecca had stolen father from mother and "lived happily ever after."

In the real world of the adult, Rebecca was very much overweight and self indulgent. Her child demanded a lot of sweets. Inside, she was sad and disappointed with the unseeing father and being "eaten up inside" by the same anger her mother had experienced living with such a father.

Rebecca at age 36 had developed a cancer similar to her mother's. Her cancer was in a state of remission and she wanted to explore variables other than medical which might help her.

She was a determined woman and still sought father's approval. So the father's F-C-C-D was explored for clues. Although much overweight, Rebecca had been addicted to sports—going to games and organizing teams and sporting events. She worked in her father's business and always felt heavy and asthmatic when going behind "the closed door" to gain father's approval—if not his love. Since her illness, Rebecca had cut down on the number of hours she worked in the father's business. Rebecca is a very creative bright person.

As she reviewed her F-C-C-Ds with father centered, Rebecca realized that all the symbols surrounding him were magnets pulling her toward him. She was being pulled in two directions—her adaptive child and her adult were in a tug-of-war creating great stress. So Rebecca decided to fight her childish desires to enter the unseeing father's space. She stayed away from sports, she gave up working for her father. Rebecca centered in her own adult world—as in Drawing 16S. She visited father's world, but consciously. Rebecca stopped

(continued on page 102)

music
love
Husband
Flowers
sisters family
Rope- pulling in two directions trying to change
Book trying to turn page
self

Drawing 16S

"Mickey Mousing around" and focused on enjoying her real, loving, seeing family and friends.

Rebecca's asthma-like episodes have cleared up. Her cancer is still in remission (one year after drawings). She has developed many more insights than her mother who took her bitterness and sadness to her grave.

Sally's F-C-C-Ds

ANOREXIC GIRL

Seventeen-year-old Sally had severe anorexia nervosa at the time she made her drawings. Sally was adopted as was her 20-year-old brother. She had been seen at age 13 with a presenting problem of slashing her arms with razor blades. At 17 she was seen for anorexia; her weight had dropped from 125 lbs to 85 lbs.

Drawing 17M. MOTHER-CENTERED

Sally's mother was shy, very proper, and very intellectualized. Adopting the children had been done at the father's insistence primarily because he wanted a "normal" family.

Mother was closer to her dog than to the children—see the Scotty dog above her head. The mother was judgmental and controlling. The hands at the top symbolize her need for control. The newspaper, books, and crossword puzzle suggest her intellectual pursuits. Food also surrounds the mother. The threatening shears close to the mother's right arm symbolize the cutting quality of this stern mother. See the marking on her arms related to Sally's attempt to control her anger with her mother. Mother was capable of conditional love. The son pleased her through his intellectual excellence. Sally was a poor student and could not meet her mother's intellectual demands. Mother wanted her to disappear.

Gardening Gloves
NY Times CROSSWORD
BOGGLE
SCRABBLE
MOM
Chocolates

Drawing 17M

Drawing 17F. FATHER-CENTERED

Sally's father was a business executive who was very conforming and proper. He was hurting in his relationship to both Sally and her mother. He said "cutting" things behind a facade of joking. Sally said she never saw affection between her parents. Notice the "clean handkerchief" above the father's head. He insisted on clean, proper behavior from his children as a condition for his love. Sally surrounds him with food and drink and power. Food is predominant in all Sally's F-C-C-Ds.

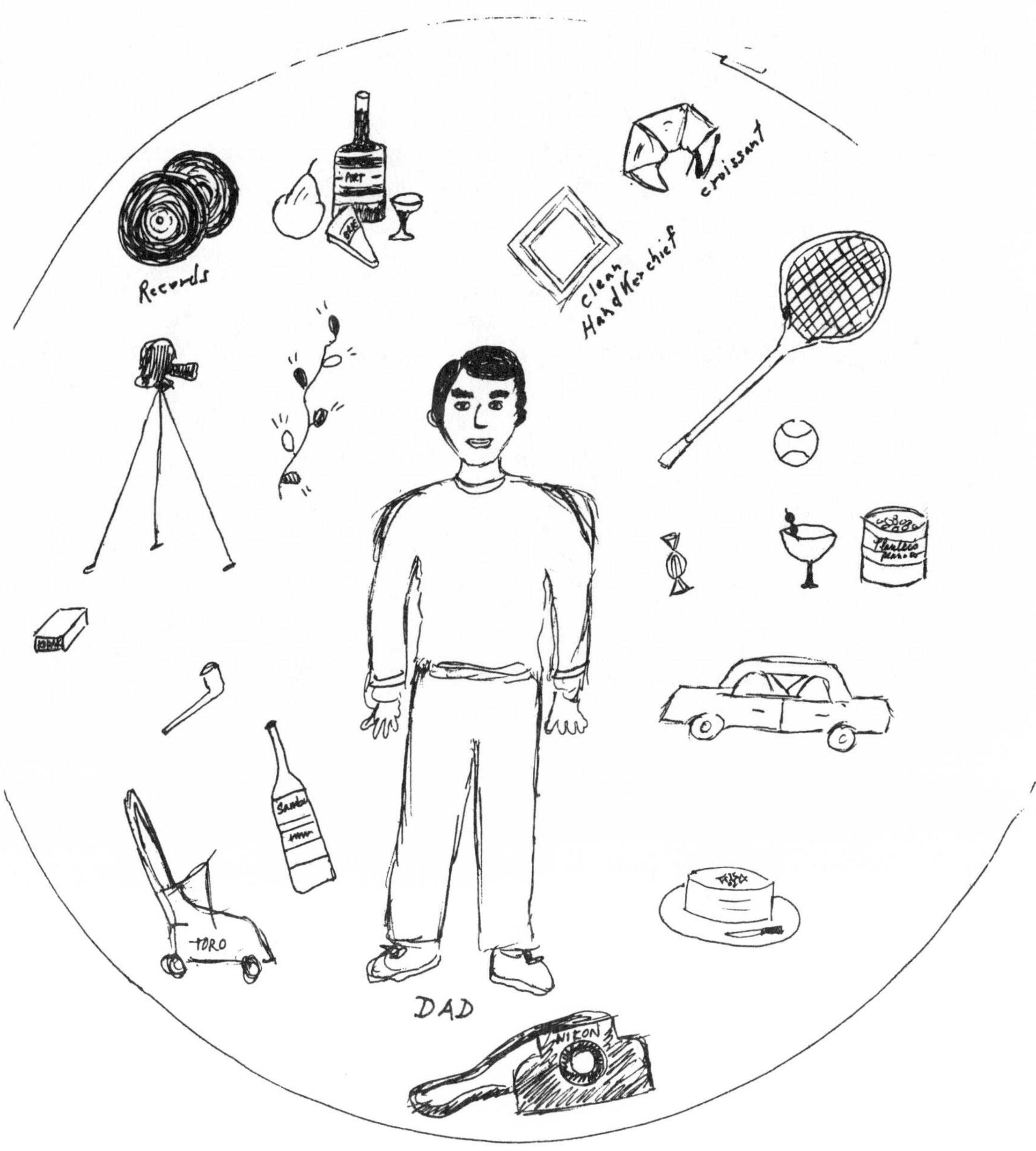

Drawing 17F

Drawing 17S. SELF-CENTERED

Food symbols lie under Sally's feet. She had numerous ritualistic behaviors related to food. For example, she would eat only three grapes at a time and counted each calorie carefully. She had exercised religiously until recently when her anorexia weakened her. The sweat clothes at the top were symptomatic of her preoccupation with her body and "keeping in shape." The zoo symbol with people watching two "big cats" probably reflected her rivalry and "cattiness" with her mother. Look at the obsessive cross-hatching of the mother's arms and the similar cross-hatching on Sally's arms—an area she once had repeatedly cut herself with razor blades. The symbolic treatment of the arms seems related to the subtle power struggle between the two cats.

Sally slowly regained her weight. Five years later she is working and self-sufficient, lives in her own apartment, has friends, and is doing well.

The dynamics revealed in Sally's F-C-C-D were helpful in formulating a treatment plan which helped Sally on her way to health.

Another technique which brings in the relationship between the parents and the self is called the Parents-Self-Centered Circle Drawing (P-S-C-D). This technique calls for placing the parents and the self in the center of a circle and visually free associating around the periphery of the circle. The drawing obtained this way is another centering technique which we explore in our next chapter.

Fortune cookie
sweat clothes
THE WRITER
school News-paper
BRUCE SPRINGSTEEN
THE RIVER
BRUCE SPRINGSTEEN
BORN IN THE USA
Bruce Springsteen Records
GUM
NOTEBOOK
ZOO
CANDY
SELF
THINGS TO DO
M
T
W
T
F
S
S
CHEESE

Drawing 17S

Chapter 3

PARENTS-SELF-CENTERED CIRCLE DRAWINGS (P-S-C-D)

Our F-C-C-Ds provide valuable information about individual figures. Placing the parents and self in the center of a drawing and free associating around the periphery gives new information. Of course we think of the three figures as external but also internalized.

INTERNAL AND EXTERNAL PARENTS AND SELF

If we view the figures as representing external, physical, "real" people, we may interpret the drawings one way.

If we view the figures as internalized, we have a richer, deeper, psychological interpretation of the P-S-C-D. The feminine and masculine forces in each of us have been called by many names: Yin and Yang in Chinese, anima and animus by Carl Jung, ida and pingala by the yoga, male and female in the west. Viewing the mother in the drawings as one manifestation of feminine energy and the father as a manifestation of masculine energy helps to enrich the possible drawing interpretations.

Some Things to Look for in a P-S-C-D

1. What person is in the center? Frequently, the centered person is in charge.

2. Relative sizes of the self compared to the parental figures. Is the self portrayed as a child? Is the self the adult and the parents children?
3. Whom is the self closest to?
4. What body language is present? Who pulls away from whom? Whose body is distorted?
5. Does the drawing reflect two and one? Who's the outsider?
6. Facial expressions: smiling, frowning, loving, and so on.
7. Does the self leave the center?
8. Is a parent removed from the center? Is there no one in the center?
9. What symbols are directly above the figures? Directly below?
10. What dominates the drawing—male or female energy?
11. Do the parents see or are their eyes blank?
12. What is omitted from the figures? Eyes? Nose? Torso? Feet?
13. What is overemphasized in the figures? Eyes? Neck? Nose? Mouth? Arms?

Placing a parent or self in the center of a drawing yields a Family-Centered Circle Drawing as discussed in Chapter two. Placing the parents and self in the center seems to probe even more deeply into the unconscious.

INSTRUCTIONS FOR OBTAINING A P-S-C-D

"Draw your parents and yourself in the middle of a circle. Try to draw a whole person, not stick people or cartoons. Surround the figures with symbols or drawings around the periphery of the circle. Visually free associate. Try to surround the central figures with symbols or drawings you associate with them."

With younger or uneducated clients the instructions may be simplified to: *"Draw your parents and yourself in the middle of a circle. Try to draw whole people, not stick people or cartoons. Doodle whatever you want around the edge of the circle."* Regular-sized typing paper ($8\frac{1}{2} \times 11$ inches) is used. The circle is predrawn on the paper and is $7\frac{1}{2}$ to 9 inches in diameter.

Our P-S-C-Ds provide another psychological tool to catch a glimpse of our psychological centers as formed in the family matrix.

Drawing 18. SARAH'S P-S-C-D: THREE-HEART SYNDROME OR OEDIPUS COMPLEX

Freud used the term Oedipus complex to refer to the boy's desire to "win" the mother from the father and the term Electra complex to refer to the girl's competition with the mother to "win" the father. More recently, psychologists use "Oedipal complex" to refer to both. Freud proposed that all people lived out the Oedipal myth. Many have talked about an Oedipal complex, but few have seen it. Our three-heart drawings provide one means of viewing the Oedipal in frozen action.

Sarah, age 46, made Drawing 18. Sarah's father was Jewish but her mother had not converted to Judaism. The star of David is above the father and the cross above the mother. The circular symbol (stomach?) above Sarah may reflect her conflicts associated with her ulcer problems. Notice the three hearts adjacent to the father, suggesting the "unresolved family romance," that is, the competition between daughter and mother for the father's attention.

In real life, Sarah and the mother "couldn't stand" one another. Jealousies and rages were frequent when they met or talked on the telephone. If the father gave any presents to Sarah, the mother would have a tantrum—sometimes fainting. Notice the necklace worn by Sarah. She had it especially made—three hearts. After the second counseling session, Sarah took off the necklace and "saw" in her drawings and necklace "the three-heart" soap opera that had been an obsession all her life.

See how close the "princess" stands to the father and how distant she is from the "ugly" mother. Sarah's P-S-C-D was an "eye-opener" for her in her journey toward maturity and wholeness.

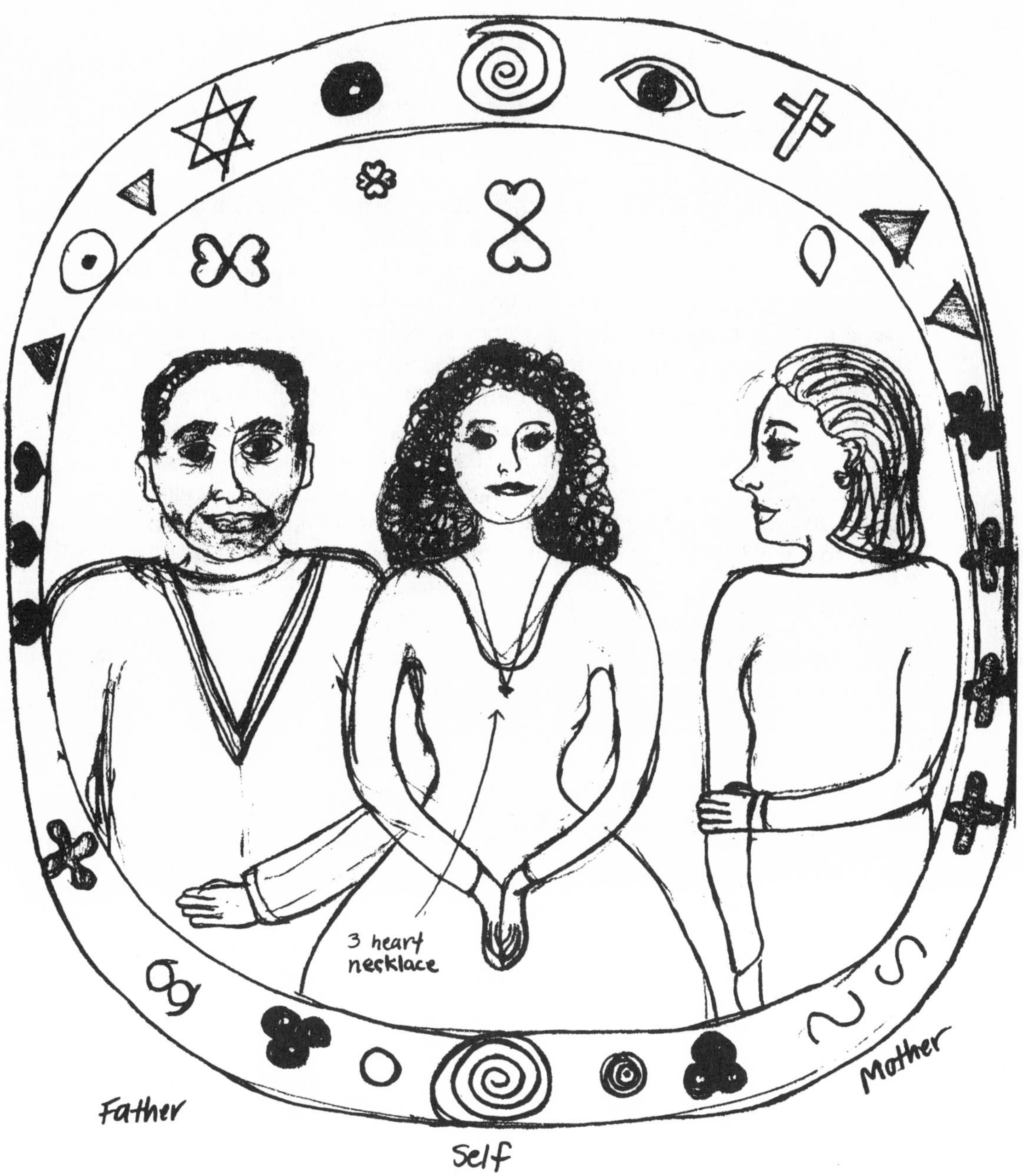
3 heart
necklace
Father
Self
Mother

Drawing 18

Drawing 19. JANE'S P-S-C-D: THREE-HEART SYNDROME, UNRESOLVED OEDIPAL

Jane, age 40, created Drawing 19. She was married and had three children. Her father had died three years prior to Drawing 19, the mother one year prior. The father had been an extremely successful businessman, greatly admired by Jane. The mother had been a mere shadow of her father. Jane never completed her family romance. She refused to compete with her mother and made herself ugly: notice the faces of the two women in the P-S-C-D. The mother holds hands with the father and is the center of the drawing.

The three hearts suggest an unfinished family romance. Jane "tilts" toward the deceased parents. She longs to join them and has many death wishes. Her unresolved family triangle has been a lifelong obsession which might have continued with her to the grave. The P-S-C-D startled Jane and opened the door to a realistic closure of her three-hearted competition.

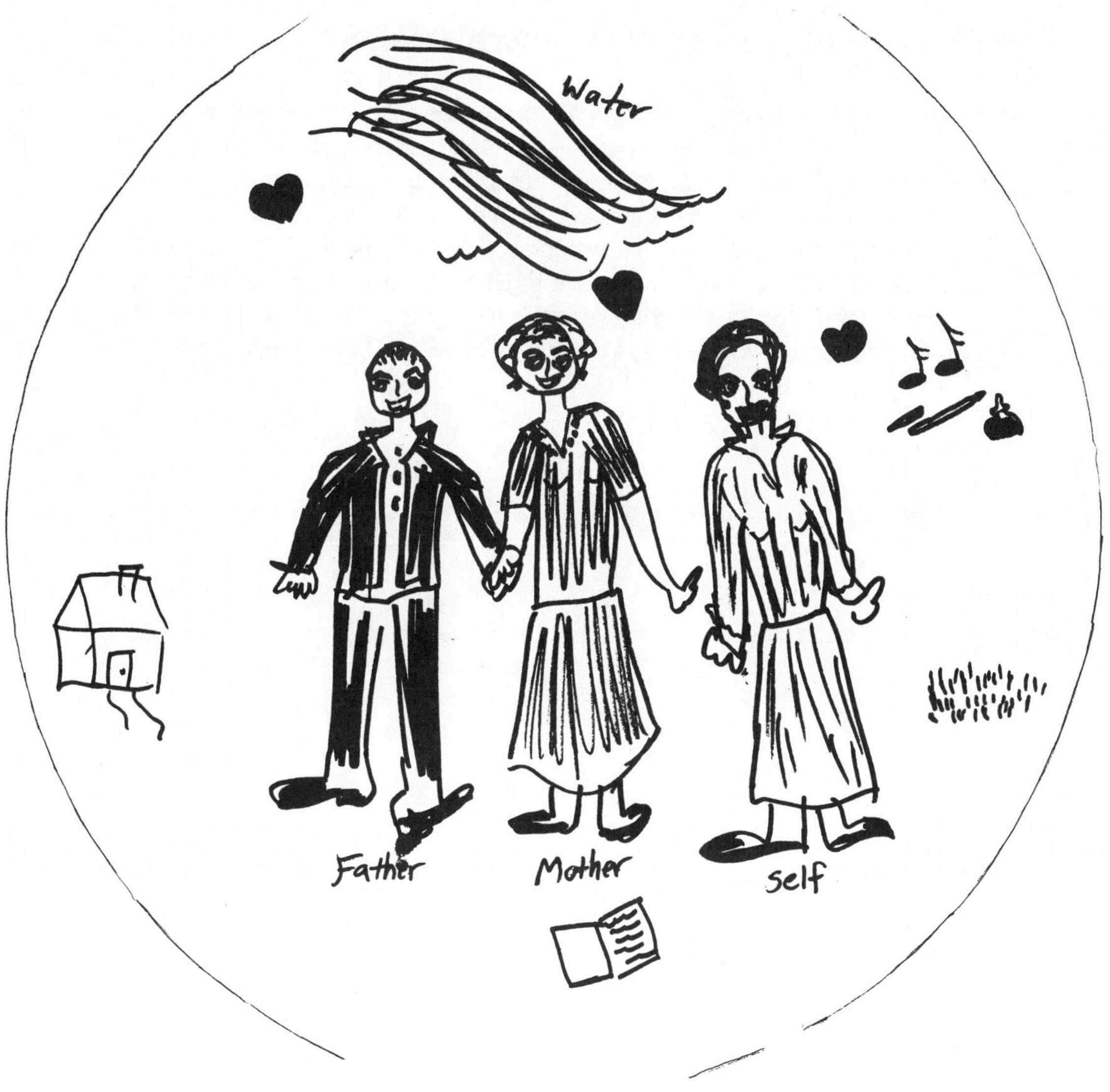
Water
Father
Mother
Self

Drawing 19

Drawing 19A. PATRICIA'S P-S-C-D: RESOLVED OEDIPAL

Patricia is 38 and Jane's younger sister. She was more assertive than Jane and "resolved" the Oedipal. Following the death of their parents, the sisters had two very different reactions. Jane wanted to follow her parents in order to resolve the family romance. Patricia has laid the parents to rest as seen in Drawing 19A. She has renewed interest in her family, two sons and two daughters, her tree of life, and music and has even taken up the game of golf. Patricia is getting on with her life. Jane is fixated and still wrestling with the three-hearted family romance—a deadly game which Jane could continue by following her parents to the grave.

HUSBAND
DAD
MOM
Self
new house
SON
daughter
Husband
SISTER
golf green

Drawing 19A

Drawing 20. DORA'S P-S-C-D: THREE-HEART SYNDROME

Dora, age 48, drew Drawing 20. Dora depicts herself as a little girl—she estimated about age 7. Dora never competed with the threatening mother for father's affection. The tight-lipped father was kept at a distance by Dora. The father had sexually molested her two sisters. Dora did not compete for his affection; her solution was to stay a little girl. The three hearts on the father's side of the drawing may reflect this unresolved problem which caused Dora much heartache as she grew older chronologically.

Dora's P-S-C-D with her three hearts provided a door-opener for her which started a growth period. She relinquished her "little girl" voice and ways.

Notice the stars on the side of the self. Stars in drawings are associated with physical and/or emotional deprivation in childhood.

Drawing 20

The star symbol has been discussed in previous K-F-D books (Burns, 1970, 1972, 1982). Here are two examples:

Drawing 21. DAVE'S K-F-D

Dave was an eight-year-old boy brought in for evaluation of his unending demands for "attention." Dave had been adopted at six months of age. Prior to this, he had been in five different foster homes and deeply deprived, according to the history. The pediatrician had told the foster mother to keep the boy at home for several months because of his general fears and unusual history. Repetitive stars in drawings are highly correlated with histories of deprivation as shown in Dave's Drawing 21.

Drawing 22. GUS'S K-F-D

Drawing 22 was taken from *Actions, Styles and Symbols in K-F-D* (Burns, 1972). This K-F-D was made by seven-year-old Gus, a boy with a history of very serious deprivation. Note the repetitive stars again, characteristic of children with histories of deprivation and usually denoting a depressive reaction to this.

Many children have told of looking at stars at night after a day of deprivation and dreaming of a better life. "When you wish upon a star—makes no difference who you are—your dreams come true."

Drawing 21

Drawing 22

Drawing 23. ANNIE'S P-S-C-D: STAR DRAWING BY JANE'S DAUGHTER

Annie, 15-year-old daughter of Jane (see Drawing 19), made Drawing 23.

Annie's mother, fixated at the "three-heart" level, was unable to meet her daughter's needs for nurturance. Note the obsessive use of stars surrounding Annie's drawing. Both her parents came from emotionally deprived families. Look at Annie's "yellow" stars above and below, apparently symbolizing a yearning for love and friendship.

Annie is in the center of her drawing and thus in more control of her life than the mother. Yet all figures are touching and Annie is caught in the web of family emotions. One suspects that without intervention Annie might display the three-heart syndrome as she "grows up."

Dad
Self
Mom
Flower
smiling face
Earth
Frown
Fern
toy alligator
Two people holding hands-friendship

Drawing 23

Drawing 24M. ANNIE'S F-C-C-D: MOTHER-CENTERED

When asked to make an F-C-C-D with her mother centered, Annie produced Drawing 24M. The woebegone expression of the mother reflects Annie's intuitive feeling that her mother is descending. The mother in a field of flowers appears to be a daughter's obsessive effort to bring beauty into her mother's space. The repetitive stars and moon are symbols seen in deprived children. Annie's poignant view of her descending, self-destructive mother gives us some idea of why she is closer to her father than to her mother.

Familiarity with symbols, such as stars, moons, horses, and hearts in Kinetic Family Drawings, as discussed in this and previous books (Burns & Kaufman, 1972; Burns, 1982, 1987) allows a richer and "deeper" understanding of the messages to be found in P-S-C-Ds.

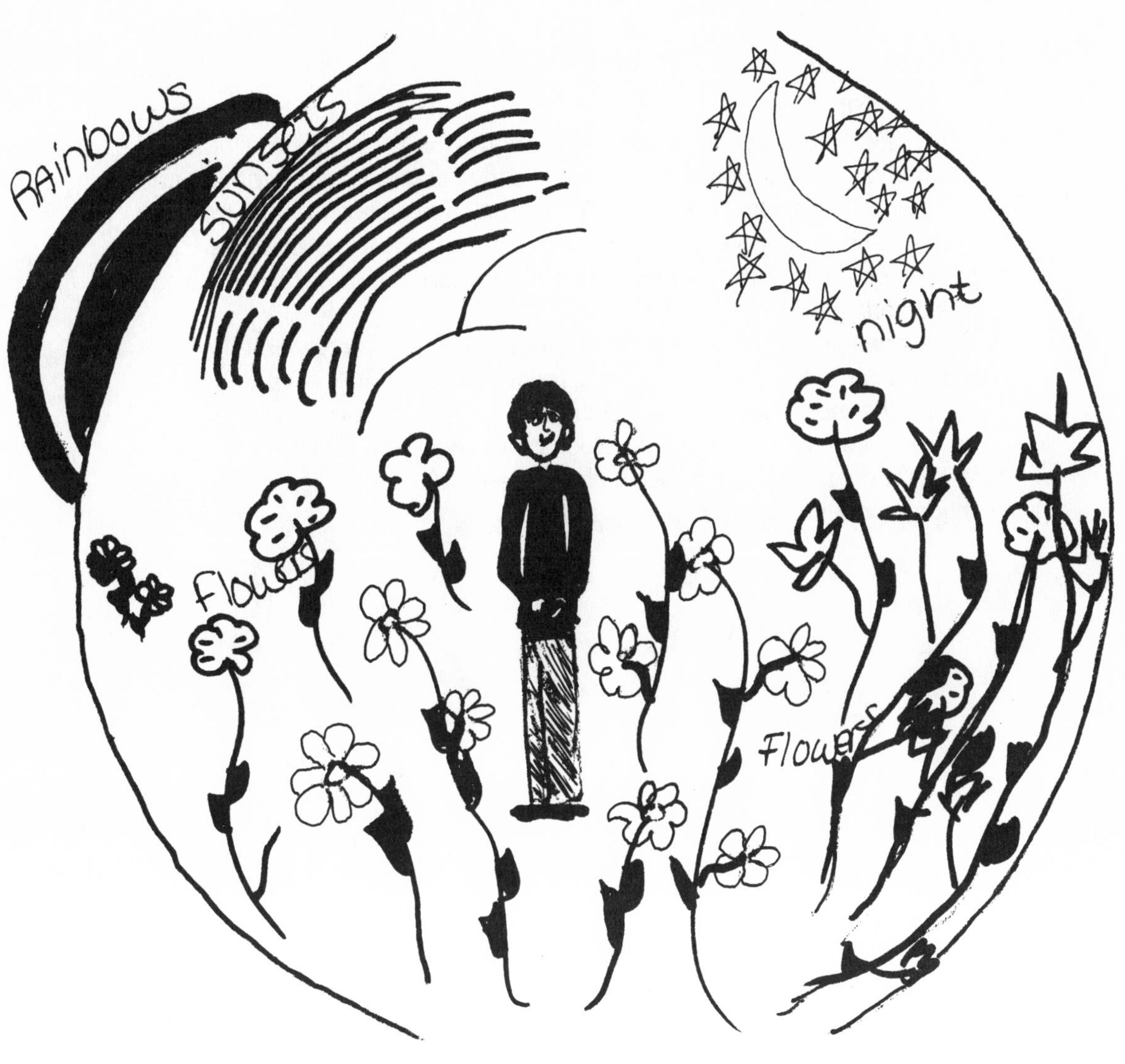
Rainbows
sunsets
night
flowers
flowers

Drawing 24M

MOONS AS SYMBOLS OF DEPRESSION

In a previous book (Burns, 1982), the symbol of snow and coldness associated with depression and suicide was discussed. Another common K-F-D symbol frequently associated with depression is the moon.

Traditionally, the sun has been viewed as the source of light and heat and consequently of life. Hence, it has been regarded as a deity and worshipped as such by all primitive peoples and has a leading place in all mythologies. Ra of the Egyptians, Helo of the Greeks, Sol of the Romans are only a few of the sun gods so worshipped.

The moon has traditionally been a symbol containing things wanted but not present on earth: unanswered prayers, fruitless love, broken vows, and so on. To cry for the moon has meant to crave for what is really beyond one's reach on earth. A lunatic is one who is moonstruck. Nothing grows in the "black light" of the cold moon. There is a high frequency of morbid moon fascination in children with unrequited love for a parent.

Drawing 25. HEIDI'S D-A-P: MOON SYMBOL AND DEPRESSION

Consider the Draw-A-Person made by 16-year-old Heidi—a wondrous portrayal of a tearful moon-maiden. Heidi has bouts of severe depression and repetitive suicidal thoughts.

Drawing 25

Drawing 26. ROGER'S K-F-D: MOON SYMBOL AND DEPRESSION

Roger's father was chronically depressed and in "dark" moods. The father is compartmentalized, separated from the family and placed in his moonstruck, "lunatic" world. Numerous other examples of the moon symbol may be found in Burns and Kaufman (1972) and Burns (1982).

Moon
Self
(going to Kitchen
to mom)
MOM
Putting flowers
in water
DAD
walking in the
moonlight
BROTHER
PAINTING
Paint

Drawing 26

Drawing 27. TOM'S P-S-C-D: STAR AND MOON SYMBOLS

Stars are one symbol frequently seen in Kinetic Drawings. Another frequent symbol is the moon. Tom's P-S-C-D has both a star and a moon. Tom was the oldest of several children. His father was childlike and ineffectual. The mother was strong-willed and ambitious. Tom tried to hold these two opposite personalities together.

The star in his P-S-C-D is above the father who is dressed all in red. In looking at the drawing, we would guess Tom is the father and Dad is the child. Tom was deprived in trying to get parenting from this immature father. Look at the mother's grim face. She was capable of giving only conditional love. See the dollar signs next to her. If Tom could be successful in getting dollars, he could get mother's conditional love. So Tom has become a "successful" workaholic.

The moon above mother's head reflected her depressed mood, partly because she was married to an unambitious, childish husband to whom she showed no warmth. Moonlight is not warm and makes nothing grow. The coffee cup above Tom reflected his need for socializing—he was always "going out for coffee" with friends. Notice the buttons on Tom. Buttons on drawings have been said to be related to dependency (Burns, 1982, pp. 244-249). Tom places the buttons on himself, reflecting his self-dependency.

Tom at age 44 was unmarried. He was capable of giving conditional love, but did not know how to receive unconditional love or to give it. Thus, he "went out" with highly ambitious, usually depressive women similar to his mother.

Yet Tom was "centered," worked hard to understand himself, and eventually allowed himself unconditional love.

Drawing 27

Drawing 28. NANCY'S P-S-C-D: DOMINANT MOTHER

Nancy, age 43, produced Drawing 28. Her father was an alcoholic who had deserted the family in Nancy's infancy. The mother never remarried and became a martyr. Nancy always felt unwanted, but clung to the few bits of affection her mother could give. The mother loved her conditionally, that is, "If you clean your room," "If you're tidy," and so on.

Mother is the center of Nancy's P-S-C-D. When Nancy finished work, she would continually question and often condemn herself: "Why weren't you nicer to that woman?" "Why didn't you smile at him?" It was as if her mother was judging Nancy's every action. Nancy was not "centered"; her mother controlled her center.

Nancy has never married. She has learned, however, to place herself in the center. This "centering" process has given her a newfound peace and control. Her P-S-C-D allowed her to see her own center and to take control of her own life.

Drawing 28

Drawing 29. PATTI'S P-S-C-D: BATTERED CHILD NEVER GREW UP

Patti, age 35, produced Drawing 29. She had a history of being battered by both parents, as was her younger sister who became lost in alcoholism. Patti married a man who battered her both physically and mentally. She remained a "little girl" as reflected in the P-S-C-D self. She doesn't want to be "touched" by her "Mom." The "mom" is distorted in that the half next to Patti is missing and "pulls away" in body language. The compartments between the figures also protect Patti. The swing above symbolizes a place to get out of the house and away from the parents. All her adult life Patti wanted out of the house and was known as a "party girl" and a "swinger." The tree with two apples suggested that she was fixated at age two (Burns, 1987). Patti was hard on herself and had not internalized a mother force to help soften her life. Patti finally left her sadistic husband, married a kinder man, and attempted to "center" herself.

Drawing 29

Drawing 30. GRETCHEN'S P-S-C-D: BATTERED CHILD RUNNING FROM PARENTS

In reviewing Drawing 30, Gretchen, age 43, said, "I can't stand placing myself near my father. He raped me when I was 11." Gretchen moved from Europe to the U.S. to escape the father. She had never told her mother or anyone about the rape episode. If we cut out the figures in Drawing 30 like paper dolls, we see how huge the father is compared to the distant self.

Even though the father and "me" are distant, Gretchen places buttons on father and self. This suggests continued "attachment" to the father.

Although escaping from the parents externally by coming to the United States, Gretchen cannot escape them internally, as may be seen in the inner world of the P-S-C-D. Running to the periphery and not being centered has caused Gretchen's problems. Although very bright, Gretchen is "not assertive" and thus limits herself. She still listens to the centered mother's dicta and thus is never satisfied with her "own" decisions.

Gretchen completed this drawing herself, analyzed the drawing herself, and appeared to derive great insight from her P-S-C-D. She was ready to begin the journey of centering.

Drawing 30

Drawing 31. LYNN'S P-S-C-D: BATTERED CHILD RETURNING HOME

Lynn, age 50, was reared by a paranoid father and a masochistic mother. The father had sexually assaulted her three brothers. The brothers had moved away and would have nothing to do with the parents. The parents were aging, with some health problems. At the time of Drawing 31, Lynn was contemplating giving up her career and returning "home" to take care of the parents. Lynn had left home at an early age and been successful in a career. She had never married.

The stars above Lynn's head suggested a deprived childhood. The explosions above the father's head represented his temper and swearing. Lynn did not know what the swirling above the mother's head meant, but thought it might symbolize confusion.

How tiny and vulnerable the little childlike self looks in Drawing 31, yet she is centered and following the mother. The self is dressed in red in contrast to the father drawn in black. Lynn planned to return "home" as the tiny adaptive child who had left some 30 years ago.

After reviewing her P-S-C-D, Lynn decided not to return home to follow in her martyred mother's footsteps. Lynn helped from a distance, but got on with her own life. Had she returned, Lynn probably would have regressed to the tiny deprived child protecting and following the mother into martyrdom.

Drawing 31

Drawing 32. CYNTHIA'S P-S-C-D: DEPRESSED MOTHER-CENTERED

Cynthia had "everything going for her," including a loving, successful husband, healthy children, many friends, and a showplace home. Only one thing was wrong: Her mother was the center of her universe, as may be seen in Drawing 32.

Cynthia's world as depicted here is colorful with tennis, family, swimming pool, flowers, and pets. The parents' side is drawn in brown. The mother attempted to "buy" love with presents—a procedure abhorred by her daughter. The couch and newspapers are symbols of the couch-potato father's abode.

The self is colorful and complete, but not centered. Cynthia's center is filled with a critical, controlling mother incapable of love without strings attached. Cynthia worked hard to become her own center and reached a point of being an observer of the parents' world without attachments.

Drawing 32

Drawing 33. GEORGE'S P-S-C-D: UNTOUCHABLE MOTHER

George, 46, had a feminine demeanor. He was successful in his professional life, but not in his social life. He has never married. George's father was a successful professional, but austere, and showed his caring through becoming a workaholic. His mother was bitter and narcissistic.

George links arms with his "Dad" in Drawing 33 but is careful not to touch his "Mom." George was out of touch with the feminine inside and outside. In the external world he had no "love affairs" with women, although he had women friends (sisters). In the internal world he did not "mother" himself and thus he was "hard" on himself. As he became older, he was turning into the person he had most denied and repressed—his mother. The huge sun above George symbolized his great need for a love he could not allow himself inwardly.

Drawing 33

Drawing 34. TIFFANY'S P-S-C-D: UNTOUCHABLE MOTHER

Tiffany, age 38, dressed like a girl of 14. She was very successful in her entrepreneur world. Tiffany was in the midst of a divorce when she made Drawing 34.

Tiffany touches her "Dad" but carefully avoids touching her "Mom." She is in touch with her masculine but not with her feminine. She is in control of the power world but not of the love world. Tiffany is a very lonely woman who denies much emotion. Her "rainbow" is missing red and orange. Her "fried egg" sun is associated with maternal deprivation.

As Tiffany worked through her divorce, she became a whole person, a person "in touch" with both her masculine and feminine components. She evolved into a woman rather than being the eternal child.

Drawing 34

Drawing 35. DON'S P-S-C-D: NO ONE IN CENTER

Don, age 49, was a highly successful executive. His father had health problems which frightened Don. The mother was controlling and "hard." Don was known in college as a "team player." In sports where he excelled the coach marveled at his ability to "sacrifice himself for his team." In his work, Don was also known as a team player. He had opportunities to be chief executive in numerous firms, but rejected these offers and remained a "second banana."

There is no central figure in Don's P-S-C-D. He functioned well in his own sunshine world. The face to his left is that of a woman he subsequently married. Don took care of his parents, but put them in a world far distant from the self. His P-S-C-D showed Don that he was not centered. Throughout his life he had allowed others to fill his vacated center.

Drawing 35

Drawing 36. JACK'S P-S-C-D: FATHER OMITTED

Jack, age 45, was a successful entrepreneur but unsuccessful in family and love matters. He had been married three times, with children from each marriage; yet Jack was a failure as a husband and a father and wondered if he could love in a home setting.

In his P-S-C-D Jack refused to include his father. He followed instructions by placing a parent in the picture, but only his mother. Jack harbored great resentment toward his father for abandoning the family when Jack was seven.

By omitting his internal father, Jack was forced to concentrate on his external masculine strivings. He was head of numerous companies and enjoyed being in the "home" office more than living in his "house." His real home he defined as a "pit stop" and his wives and children resented his absence. Perhaps the three mountains and three trees surrounding Jack's P-S-C-D reflected his need for a unity of mother, father, self.

Drawing 36

Drawing 37. MATHEW'S P-S-C-D: UNSEEING PARENTS

Note Mathew's piercing eyes and how they contrast with the blank, unseeing eyes of his parents. Mathew felt his parents never really looked at him with compassion.

Notice how he reaches out and touches the parents, but they pull away—particularly the mother. Look at the distortion on the side of the mother adjacent to the self; her body language pulls her away from her son.

See the waves on either side of the circle. Water in our P-S-C-Ds in our western culture usually symbolizes sadness-tears. Note the paisley teardrops adjacent to the mother. Note the moons above Mathew and his father and the sun beyond the waves above the mother. The flowers on the outer upper periphery suggest Mathew's strengths in moving upward toward them.

Mathew is in the process of ascending above his nongiving parents. When he lets them go and creates his new internal nurturing parents, he will be free to grow.

Flowers
pluses and minuses
water-waves
suns
MOONS
polka-Dots
triangles
paisley-tear-drops
Mother
Father
Self

Drawing 37

Drawing 38. JENNY'S P-S-C-D: ATTACHMENT TO MOTHER

Jenny, age 20, is somewhat "slow" but has worked hard to find self-sufficiency. She is an only child and attached to her mother.

In her P-S-C-D, the lines attaching "Mom and me" reflect Jenny's symbiosis. Notice how much bigger Mom's head is. When decisions are made, Jenny looks to Mom. The mother had tried valiantly to help Jenny build self-confidence. When the attachment to mother is over and the psychological umbilical cord is cut, Jenny will be ready to "move out."

Drawing 38

Drawing 38A. JENNY'S P-S-C-D: FREEDOM FROM ATTACHMENT

Jenny's P-S-C-D drawn two years after Drawing 38 reflects her growth. The lines attaching Jenny to mother are gone. The self has moved away from Mom. Notice how the eyes have enlarged; Jenny now "sees" more clearly. She is now 22 and reminds everyone that she expects to be treated as an adult.

In our next chapter, we will show how Symbol-Centered Probes (SYM-C-P) and doodle probes may be used to uncover positive and negative symbols.

Drawing 38A

Chapter 4

SYMBOL-CENTERED PROBES (SYM-C-P) AND DOODLE PROBES

A foreign object in the body, such as a piece of glass, is surrounded, encapsulated, and ejected. Just so, it seems, a traumatic psychological happening, such as a rape, is surrounded, encapsulated, and ejected from the mind/body.

The use of Symbol-Centered Probes (SYM-C-P) may allow a person to travel into the labyrinth of the mind in a very short time. In the labyrinthine journey, symbols may be found along the way which block growth. For harmony to be achieved, these symbols must be seen, understood, and dissolved so that a person may continue his/her journey. Discovery of positive symbols may enhance growth and healing.

Consider the drawings of Marie, age 18. Marie had been seen by a variety of "talking" therapists during a five-year period. She had vague presenting problems such as general malaise, mood swings, anxiety attacks, and somatic complaints. Although very bright, Marie was not doing well in school. She seemed chronically unhappy and ill at ease.

Marie was asked to make a Kinetic-House-Tree-Person drawing (Burns, 1987) and produced Drawing 39.

Knotholes in tree drawings have been likened to "whirlpools" of the mind (Burns, 1987), usually depicting a psychological trauma surrounded and encapsulated in the tree of life. Marie made a knothole in her tree drawing with an owl inside.

Drawing 39. MARIE'S K-H-T-P DRAWING

Drawing 39A. MARIE'S SYMBOL PROBE: KNOTHOLE-CENTERED

Marie was asked to center this knothole-owl in a circle. She produced Drawing 39A. She started with the eyes and then Jim, a man who had raped her five years previously, appeared.

(continued on page 156)

Marie had never "talked to" her parents or therapists about Jim. In two sessions using the K-H-T-P drawing and a symbol probe, Marie was able to "see" into the encapsulated knothole-owl symbol and transform this symbol into Jim the rapist. By bringing the encapsulated trauma into conscious *visual* awareness, she was able to cast out the encapsulated hurt.

With a few supportive sessions, Marie was healed. Two years later, Marie is symptom-free and attending a major university where she is doing well academically and socially.

Carl Jung spoke of tree drawings as a profile view of the self- and circle-centered drawings as a symbol of the self seen in cross section (Metzner, 1981). For Jung, the symbol served as a bridge between levels of consciousness.

Drawing 40. HAL'S P-S-C-D: ALCOHOLIC SON OF A REJECTING FATHER

Hal, age 22, was deeply troubled at the time he made this drawing. His arms and wrists were scarred. When drunk he would smash windows and come close to destroying himself.

Hal's parents had divorced when he was eight. His father had remarried and "rejected" him. He was unwelcome in the father's home, but welcome in the mother's.

Note the small self figure between the parents. Both parents are smiling, but the self is not. Hal is attempting to identify with the father (shading of figure and shape). The adjoining sides of the father and son figures are broken at the shoulder, perhaps reflecting the incomplete or "broken" relationship. The mother figure is whole without breaks.

The "fried egg" sun is above the mother. This fried egg symbol is frequent in other projectives such as the Rorschach and is correlated with emotional deprivation in childhood. The symbols adjacent to the mother are feminine and "empty," usually a positive sign in that they are receptive and may be filled. The maternal grandparents' house at the bottom symbolized home and caring to Hal. He visited them sporadically during his childhood and had fond memories of them.

(continued on page 158)

sun
Box
MOM SELF DAD
Airmap to Arizona
Grandparents House
Pool
child-person
Jagged Rocks

Drawing 40

Adjacent to the father we see a flower—similar to the "fried egg" sun and perhaps reflecting a desire to be loved by dad. The arrows are symbols of hurting or anger, pointing to the sun circling toward the "child-person" at the bottom. Hal said he often "doodled" and this figure emerged; a child person battered on jagged rocks. The person-child resembles a tombstone, perhaps associated with Hal's death wishes.

Drawing 40A. HAL'S SYM-C-P: BATTERED CHILD WITH DEATH WISHES

When we reviewed Drawing 40 with Hal, he felt the child-person battered on the rocks was the source of much suffering. Hal was asked to place the child-person-on-rocks in Drawing 40A and surround it with symbols. It was as if we were penetrating to a deeper or more unconscious layer of Hal's psyche and trying to bring the diseased area into the healing light of consciousness.

Around the top areas of the circle in Drawing 40A, Hal drew stars—a deprivation symbol not seen in Drawing 40. He described the boat at the top as symbolizing his lack of direction—a tiller but no tiller-person—floating, helpless, directionless. The wheel symbolized "going round in circles" without direction. The arrow symbolized his anger, as in Drawing 40. The long highway moving into the foothills symbolized his desire to be nurtured. The foothills seemed breast symbols and the long road leading to them his

(continued on page 160)

wheel
rising
sun
ME
geometrical
shapes
buildings

Drawing 40A

obsession with being nurtured. The sun is rising and warming the stars and the battered child. The geometrical shapes were male and female sexual symbols which he felt were related to his relationship to his girlfriend. The city building symbolized the stresses of the city—stresses the little battered child wanted to avoid and did so by drinking and trying to forget the suffering of abandonment.

Hal "got in touch" with his battered child by probing deeper into his unconscious and finding the source of his sickness.

The next stage was to incorporate the battered child gently into Hal's adult life. Hal did this rather quickly. He developed a much better, less intense relationship with his girlfriend, Sue. Sue had been afraid of Hal and could intuit the anger in him if his dependency needs were not met. She became a friend and nurturer to the battered child who no longer controlled Hal unconsciously. Hal entered law school, gave up drinking, and seems to be on his way to a balanced, reasonable life with Sue. He found his battered child deep in his unconscious and brought him out into the healing sun of the real world.

Drawing 41. GERALDINE'S P-S-C-D

Geraldine, age 39, had doodled a dragon since childhood. Her P-S-C-D, Drawing 41, gave us some clues as to the meaning of the doodle.

Note how the self is separated from the boxed parents. No one in the drawing has a nose. Noses are associated with anger. Large noses (pig or bull like) suggest anger (snorting) directed outward. Absence of nostrils suggests anger directed inward. Geraldine mentioned that no one in the family dared show any anger in the presence of this cutting father. Notice the explosion outside the box between self and mother. Geraldine had learned to implode anger.

Drawing 41

Drawing 42. GERALDINE'S DRAGON DOODLE

Geraldine was asked to center the dragon in a circle and surround it with symbols. Drawing 42 appeared. Note the huge dragon nostrils in contrast to the no-nostril family figures. See the symbols surrounding the dragon—the stars, so frequently seen in our drawers who were deprived as children. The lightning is associated with striking out in anger. The rug reflects a role Geraldine played within a family. She allowed people to walk on her rather than expressing forbidden anger toward them. Geraldine married two men who walked on her as did her children. The meaning of the symbols surrounding the dragon became clear to Geraldine: Stars—lightning—rug symbolized deprivation, anger, obsequious behavior.

Geraldine "saw" this relationship quickly and finally had some understanding of her compulsive dragon doodling.

Drawing 42

Drawing 43. RICHARD'S SYM-C-P: TOTEM POLE DOODLE-CENTERED

Richard, age 36, was seen with his wife, Marian. She complained that he had an obsession with totem poles. He had doodled totem poles since childhood and compulsively collected them in all sizes. Their house and backyard were crowded with totem poles.

Richard's totem pole doodle was centered by him in a symbol probe. The totem pole was in the form of a bird and surrounded by father-son, a radio, and a sailing boat.

Richard had had a lonely childhood. The father had left the family when Richard was six. The mother worked and Richard was frequently home alone. The radio became his friend and contact with people. Marian complained that he played it constantly inside and outside the home. Once Richard's father bought him a toy sailboat which he fondly remembered.

The highlight of Richard's relationship with his father was a trip to a museum in which they saw a display of totem poles. Thus, the totem became the symbol of Richard's obsessive attempts to be close to his father. Seeing his doodle probe helped Richard to become free from his childish attachment to a lost dad.

Drawing 43

Chapter 5

THE CENTERING PROCESS AS SHOWN IN KINETIC DRAWINGS

"Centering: that act which precedes all others on the potter's wheel. The bringing of the clay into a spinning, unwobbling pivot, which will then be free to take innumerable shapes as potter and clay press against each other."

—M. C. RICHARDS (1962)

Like most people I know, I am fascinated by symbols of balance and wholeness. Centering is one image to symbolize the process of becoming a balanced person. Richards' metaphor of the similarity between creating pottery and creating people is poetic and yet such a metaphor can unite disciplines.

We have tried to show that people who place themselves in the center of a P-S-C-D tend to be better balanced than those with the self not centered. In this chapter we will explore one woman's journey toward a non-attached, balanced centering. During the course of her journey, this woman was given a series of drawings to do including a Kinetic-Shop-Window Drawing, a Kinetic-House-Tree-Person Drawing, several Family-Centered Circle Drawings, and a Parents-Self-Centered Drawing.

INSTRUCTIONS FOR OBTAINING A KINETIC-SHOP-WINDOW DRAWING

Kinetic-Shop-Window Drawings (K-S-W-D) are useful in obtaining a cross section of symbols.

The instructions are a form of guided imagery. "*You are in a strange city and exploring. You come to this interesting area, turn the corner and in the distance see a shop window. As you approach the window, you are fascinated by the contents. Draw the shop window. Try to put at least three things in the window.*" After completing the K-S-W-D, the drawer is told that each of the objects or figures in the window may come to life and talk to the examiner. Drawings are done on standard typing paper ($8\frac{1}{2} \times 11$ inches).

INSTRUCTIONS FOR OBTAINING A KINETIC-HOUSE-TREE-PERSON DRAWING

Kinetic-House-Tree-Person Drawings (K-H-T-P) help to define many growth variables (Burns, 1987).

The instructions for obtaining the K-H-T-P are: "Draw a house, a tree, and a whole person on this piece of paper with some kind of action. Try to draw a whole person, not a stick or cartoon figure." Drawings are done on standard typing paper ($8\frac{1}{2} \times 11$ inches).

Maria's Centering Journey

Drawing 44. MARIA'S KINETIC-SHOP-WINDOW DRAWING (K-S-W-D): DEPRESSION, REGRESSION, AND HOPELESSNESS

Maria, age 34, is a very talented woman. She excels in music and art but has not "found herself." She had periods of depression and often considered suicide. Her father was a traveling salesman, disconnected from the family and unable to love them. The family consisted of mother, father, and three sisters. The mother was immature and had a vicious temper, competed with the sister for love, was talented but unfulfilled, and had a tendency toward depression and martyrdom.

Maria had been married and was following in her mother's footsteps. Her husband was immature, obsessed with being cared for, and unable to give much love. One day Maria decided to end her childless seven-year marriage and start her journey toward growth and fulfillment. She changed her name from Carol to Maria. Drawing 44 reflects Maria's starting point in her journey.

In Drawing 44, the three baby dolls in the window said they had been there for a long time, nobody wanted them. The shop was closed. It had been a junk shop but the 70-year-old male owner hadn't sold much and had given up. The door was to keep people out. The vase and wheat emblem at the top were symbols of pride in the past.

The whole junk shop story was one of depression, hopelessness, and surrender reflecting the depth of Maria's discouragement at the time of the drawing.

Drawing 44

Drawing 45. MARIA'S KINETIC-HOUSE-TREE-PERSON DRAWING (K-H-T-P): THE BEGINNINGS OF GROWTH AND OF NURTURING OTHERS

Two weeks after completing Drawing 44, Maria made Drawing 45, a K-H-T-P drawing. The central figure, the self, is down on her knees tending the garden. In having the objects in the picture come to life, the flowers became her family—three sisters and two parents. The colorless flower tended by Maria was symbolic of the father and her attempt to care for a father whose spirit had faded. The cat was symbolic of the ever-watching "catty" competitive sister/mother "overseeing" Maria's gardening. The mighty tree reflects inner strengths and creative energies. Maria had grown from a helpless baby in Drawing 44 to a helpful human being in Drawing 45, albeit still on her knees.

Drawing 45

Drawing 46. MARIA'S F-C-C-D: MOTHER-CENTERED

The sun in Drawing 46 is setting—often a symbol of sadness as daylight diminishes. The tree tends to move downward. The mother is surrounded by food and nurturing. The paintbrush is a symbol associated with her artistic talent. The bright scarf (a type very frequently worn by Maria) brightens her space. The bird symbol of movement upward is near the top. Maria cheers up her mother's world.

The tiny figure in the bottom right quadrant is felt by Maria to be herself, stretched out, hoping for warmth from the setting sun—a helpless, cross-like baby doll. The skis and poles, symbols of coldness, are crossed with the ski pole loops hanging above the "baby," suggestive of nooses. Maria gives her all to the immature mother, but gets no sunshine in return.

Drawing 46

Drawing 47. MARIA'S F-C-C-D: FATHER-CENTERED

How small the father is compared to Maria's large portrait of her mother. At the top are books, perhaps symbolic of the book world preferred by the father. A drink is kindly offered by the hand (Maria's?). Maria tries to comfort her unfeeling father who is glued to his book or TV or absent in his car. The fried egg symbol next to the father is seen in drawings by people deprived in their childhood.

Psychologically Maria's father was missing. Even so, she gave her love to him, but received very little back. The crumbs of father love were fought for by the sisters and child/mother, resulting in violent jealousies and "cattiness."

Drawing 47

Drawing 48. MARIA'S F-C-C-D: SELF-CENTERED

Compare Maria's face with that of her mother as seen in Drawing 46. Maria makes her face plain and homely in contrast to the beautiful face she gives the mother. She felt sorry for her mother and, as do many loving daughters, Maria refused to compete with her, letting her mother win the pathetic competition for father's affection. Maria had many wonderful qualities, being warm, thoughtful, and friendly as reflected in the stance and welcoming gesture of the self figure. The sun is rising and the tree is moving upward. The self is not a baby nor down on her knees, but upright and hopeful. Yet see the dark, tiny figure floating on the water, seeking sunshine. This figure suggests a shadow-self, depressed and needy—about the same size and dressed like the pathetic little figure awaiting sunshine portrayed in the mother-centered F-C-C-D (Drawing 46).

On the left side of the self figure are wavy colors, which Maria identified as feelings. Maria is "attached" to her feelings. The clarinet on the tree reminds her of playing the clarinet in the high school band.

The bicycle apparently reflects her desire to escape. Maria has always felt a Gypsy-urge to move about like a butterfly searching for love and beauty.

Nothing in the father-centered Drawing 47 is repeated in the self-centered drawing, but symbols from the mother-centered drawing are repeated in the self drawing—the bird, the sun, the tree, the tiny figure seeking warmth, the water. Maria is more comfortable in the mother's world, but starved for warmth—a "deprived" child.

Drawing 48

Drawing 49. MARIA'S PARENTS-SELF-CENTERED DRAWING (P-S-C-D): CENTERING AND FREEDOM

Some two months later, Maria produced Drawing 49. She depicts herself controlling the puppet parents. She is whole—the parents incomplete. In a beauty contest, she and the mother might be equal. The bird is large and flying high as was Maria on her spiritual quest. The "stars" below her, suggestive of deprivation in childhood, are present but distant. The swirling emotions still are present, but Maria is rising above them and dancing. Her tree of life is still powerful, alive, and growing.

Maria is centered and balanced and beautiful and whole and "soaring"—she is beginning her journey to self-realization.

Drawing 49

Chapter 6

CONCLUSIONS

Family-Centered Circle Drawings (F-C-C-D) provide a technique for the drawer to see each parent and the self more clearly. When visual free associations are made around each of the figures, symbols appear, both positive and negative, associated with the father, mother, and self.

In Parents-Self-Centered Drawings (P-S-C-D), the relation of the self to father and mother is seen more clearly. Do the parents see the self? Do they touch the self lovingly? Do they pull away? Do they drive the self from the center? Those drawers who portray a nonnurturing critical parent whom they refuse to touch or be close to are frequently "out of touch" with their internalized parent. If you are not "in touch" with your internal nurturing mother, how can you nurture and love yourself? If you are "out of touch" with your internal nurturing father, how can you find security and stability within?

Consider the massive denial portrayed in drawings throughout this book. Faces are missing. Body parts are missing or distorted. Whole people are missing. Where there is massive denial of parents, family, or self, shadow people roam. Many drawers with abhorrent feelings about parents find themselves slowly turning into the parents. It is as if the long-repressed shadow personality gains control. But creative shadows of people suppressed by parents or society or self may break out.

Study of human figure drawings helps point out areas of denial. Recognition and removal of the denial can release healing energy, allowing the person to grow.

In viewing a P-S-C-D, we see not just a mother, father, self drawing, but feminine and masculine energy moving—not just in the left or right brain but throughout the person.

For example, if we have a very large mother in the P-S-C-D, we assume a feminine energy dominates the drawer. The drawer is "out of balance." Until the male and female energy is balanced within, the whole centered self cannot rise. Growth will be blocked until this balance and harmony are obtained at each level of consciousness.

Of course, we view the mother and the father in the P-S-C-D as psychological parents, not just physical parents. For example, the mother in a P-S-C-D might include mother, stepmother, grandmother, aunts, sisters, babysitters, female teachers, cultural views on femininity, genetic and hormonal factors—a composite we call a psychological mother-feminine energy.

Here are some of the more frequent negative qualities seen in the Family-Centered Circle Drawings.

QUALITIES SEEN IN UNHEALTHY INTERNALIZED PARENTS AND SELF DRAWINGS

1. People with features or parts omitted.
2. Distortion and out-of-proportion sizes of mother, father, or self.
3. Unfriendly faces or missing parts.
4. A parent is centered or the center is vacant.
5. Members are attached or widely distanced.
6. Body language shows parents or self pulling away or guarded.
7. Parents not looking at self. No eyes or turned away.
8. Surrounding symbols are negative.
9. Drawing depicts a world in which you would not like to live.

Specific Omission or Overemphasis in F-C-C-Ds

1. Omission of eyes or pupils in eyes depicts an unseeing (uncaring) person.
2. Omission of nose indicates inability to project anger outward. Usually comes from people reared in families where anger is not acceptable. "No fighting here."
3. Omission of mouth suggests inability to express dependency or weakness. "Big boys (or girls) don't cry."
4. Omission of neck suggests "bull-headedness" seen in strong-willed people.

5. Omission of arms is associated with a fear of power.
6. Omission of body below waist shows sexual denial.
7. Omission of feet shows instability and a "Gypsy" personality.

Overemphasis

1. Of eyes: hypervigilance.
2. Of nose: anger turned outward; bull- or piglike nostrils, and so on.
3. Of mouth: dependency.
4. Elongated neck: dependency; giraffe neck.
5. Elongated arms: need for power and control.
6. Elongated feet: need for stability, security.

QUALITIES SEEN IN HEALTHY INTERNALIZED PARENTS AND SELF DRAWINGS

1. Whole people; no body feature omitted or distorted.
2. Balance in size of father, mother, and self and bodily parts.
3. Seeing, friendly faces with eyes, nose, and mouth on parents and self.
4. The self is centered and in control.
5. The members are not attached, not touching, but standing on own two feet.
6. Body language showing openness and not pulling away. Parents are symmetrical and not distorted on side adjacent to self.
7. Ideally, parents are looking at and seeing self.
8. Surrounding symbols, particularly directly above parents and self, are positive and hopefully soaring.
9. Depict a world in which you would like to live.

In general, if the inner parents are positive, then activate them. If the inner parents are negative, then recreate them in a positive form, center yourself, and take charge of your growth.

Figure 1. Normal, Healthy P-S-C-D

Drawing 50. BETTY'S P-S-C-D: BECOMING A WHOLE-CENTERED PERSON

Betty, age 35, is far advanced on her own journey of completeness. She is warm, wise, and appreciated by most people. She is loving to herself and others.

In her P-S-C-D drawing, Betty allows her parents their own space. She says the flames to the right of the self are "burning through," opening up a new world for her where she will be centered as a whole person on her own journey. Transformation is often symbolized by the element of fire. Fire is associated with the emotion of purification or simplification, the dissolving of old problems or barriers.

"Because I am a potter, I take my image, centering, from the potter's craft. A potter brings clay into center on the potter's wheel and then gives it whatever shape he/she wishes. The potter fires the kiln, partly from hellfire, fire of suffering, fire from which the phoenix rises, the purifying fire—the final form taken."

—(RICHARDS, 1962)

Drawing 50

As the acorn becomes the oak, so too must the individual rise from its acorn beginnings by releasing the parents of origin and breaking into its own space.

If the original parents are nurturing and balanced, they may be incorporated into internal parents. If the original parents are not nurturing and conducive to growth, the individual must touch and internalize the best of the female and male models in his/her life and *create his/her own inner parents.*

When this process is complete, the individual, balanced and growing, may get in touch with the higher realms of self-realization.

Figure 2. Journey in Creation of Inner Parents: From Acorn to Oak

SARA PORTER 89

APPENDIX
Frequent Symbols in Kinetic and Family Circle Drawings

Certain symbols recur in our K-F-Ds and F-C-C-Ds and are considered to be important and worthy of discussion because of their recurrence and consistent association with clinical material.

Bikes: Bicycling is a common activity. In family drawings, the bicycle suggests wheels upon which the person may move into a new space. Thus, a bicycle moving out of the drawing has different meaning than one moving into the center of the drawing. The latter movement is rare. During adolescence the power of the bike and motorbike becomes particularly important in reinforcing masculine strivings.

Books: Books placed at the midline of the body are often feminine sexual symbols (Burns, 1982). Books in other places are usually books, but may be displaced sexual symbols.

Brooms: The broom is a recurrent symbol, particularly in the hands of a parent (usually the mother) who puts emphasis on household cleaning as a reflection of conditional love, i.e. "If you're clean in body and mind, I can love you." The "witchy" mother frequently carries a broom.

Butterflies: This symbol is associated with the search for illusive love and beauty.

Buttons: Buttons on individuals are associated with attachment to or dependency upon the figure in which they appear. Buttons on the self suggest self dependency.

Cats: Sometimes cats are cats, but often they are symbolic of feminine rivalry where individuals tend to be "catty" or childishly jealous and rivalrous.

Christmas Trees: A frequently recurring symbol found in drawings of those with a history of deprivation and a deep desire to find the "spirit of Christmas."

Clowns: A symbol frequently seen in those wishing to cheer up those around them.

Often seen in those brought up in homes with mental or physical illness. The drawer has a desire to make others happy, especially others who are depressed.

Drums: A symbol found in the drawings of those who have difficulty in expressing anger openly and thus displace their anger onto the drum.

Electricity: This symbol is usually associated with extreme need for warmth and love. There is an element of control and, at times, anger if these needs are not met.

Fire: There are at least three meanings associated with fire as a symbol: (1) The intense need for warmth and love; (2) The fact that love may turn into hate is also reflected in the fire, often seen as a destructive force; (3) Fire may symbolize a transformational energy—a "burning through" to a new level of development.

Flowers: Flowers represent love of beauty and the growth process. In little girls, the flower drawn below the waist suggests feminine identification.

Fried Egg: A repetitive symbol found in the drawings of those with significant childhood deprivation. See further discussion under Sun.

Heat: Heat in all forms—sunshine, light, lamps, lightbulbs, electricity, fire, etc.—symbolizes the need for warmth and love.

Heart: Usually a symbol of love. Sometimes a concern about a "heart condition" may be present. Three hearts drawn together suggest an unresolved "family romance."

Hooks: Hooks of various kinds, including hangers, are often symbolic of acute pain associated with various traumatic happenings.

Horses: At puberty and early adolescence many girls "love" horses. When asked why, they often say, "They're the most beautiful animal and people like to ride them." The safe, comfortable, sexual symbolic identification seems universal in western culture.

Jump Ropes: Jump ropes often encapsulate a person disturbing to the drawer.

Kites: Kites and sometimes balloons are symbolic of an attempt to "rise above" a situation to a higher level of development.

Ladders: Symbol of tension and precarious balance when leaning against something.

Lamps: Lamps are a symbol of warmth and love.

Leaves: Leaves are a symbol of dependency: They cling to their source of nurturance and are unable to survive without attachment.

Moon: A recurrent symbol in our drawings associated with depression. It has traditionally been a symbol containing things wanted but not present on earth.

Mountains: Mountains have a variety of meanings. They are frequently seen in drawings of dependent people where they may be breast symbols. They may also be symbols of strength and permanence and upward search.

Necks: Necks are one of the more reliable and clinically valid features of human figure drawings. Long necks are associated with dependency. Short- or non-neck drawings are associated with independence or "bullheadedness."

Noses: Noses are another reliable and clinically valid feature of human figure drawings. Large noses or prominent nostrils (pig nose, bull nose) are associated with anger directed outward. No nose is associated with anger directed inward.

Rain: Rain is a recurrent feature associated with sadness or depression (tear drops). Frequently the rain will be falling on a particular person.

Refrigerators: Associated with coldness and deprivation with accompanying depression.

Rugs: Symbols of servility and "walked upon qualities" associated with masochism.

Skin Diving: Excessive preoccupation with skin diving and other underwater activities is associated with withdrawal and depressive tendencies. When teenaged boys are asked about this preoccupation, they often say that when under water they cannot hear nor interact with the parents, particularly the father. Poignantly depicted in the underwater scenes in the movie, *The Graduate.*

Snakes: In the West, the snake as a phallic symbol is so well known in the literature that discussion is unnecessary. In the East, the snake may be a symbol of rejuvenation (shedding the skin) and of male (yang) power.

Snow: Snow is a frequent symbol in projectives, including the Rorschach, of significant depression, especially, of course, in people living in no-snow country or in a drawing made at a time of year without snow. Snow is frozen water, psychologically often symbolic of frozen tears.

Stars: A frequent symbol drawn by those with a history of physical or emotional deprivation. Deprived people often recall a childhood in which, following a deprived period, they "wished upon a star" for a better life.

Stop Signs: Stop signs or "Keep Out" signs seem obvious attempts at impulse control.

Sun: The sun is a symbol of warmth and growth. The style used in drawing the sun tells much about the drawer's attempt to find love. For example:

Suns: Suns are one of the more frequent symbols used at all developmental levels. The type of sun reflects how the individual allows warmth or love into their world. The size of the sun reflects the amount of warmth the individual wants. Who is the sun close to in the drawing? Whose head is it over? Who receives the rays? Here are some frequently drawn types of suns.

Aggressive Sun. Drawn by those who reach out and insist upon sunshine.

Broken Ray Sun. Individual wants warmth but doesn't follow through.

Compulsive Sun. People who draw suns this way tend to be organized and compulsive in trying to get love. They may try to be neat and orderly and "perfect" in seeking conditional warmth.

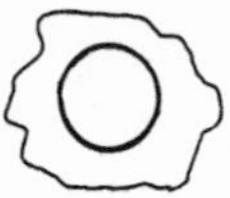

Encapsulated Sun: The "fried egg sun." A frequent symbol in those with a history of physical or mental deprivation. Warmth is not allowed in nor radiated out.

Passive Sun. Drawn by passive people who do not reach out for warmth or love.

Swirling Sun. Drawn by those obsessed with the need for warmth. A whirlpool in their mind.

Unbroken Rays. Drawn by people who reach out for warmth and follow through in this effort.

Trees: In general, the tree is a symbol of individual growth ranging from dead-appearing trees to lively, vital-appearing trees. Knotholes in trees may reflect "whirlpools" of the mind where unresolved traumas "spin" around. Analysis of tree drawings has been described in Buck and Hammer (1969) and Burns (1987).

Vacuums: The symbol of the vacuum or other cleaning tools, i.e. brooms, mops, etc., are associated with a need for cleanliness and order. The drawer has usually come from a family in which love is conditional, i.e. "If you're clean and neat, you are lovable."

Water: Overexaggeration and preoccupation with water is associated with depression. Often a focal depression is seen in water involving one person. A drawing may be filled with cheery sunshine or gloomy rain, reflecting the mood of the drawer.

X's: The "X" seems a universal symbol of conflict, ambivalence, and an attempt to control. Sometimes the "X" means "stop." The symbol is often hidden in the matrix of the drawing.

REFERENCES

BUCK, J. W. and HAMMER, E. F. (Eds.) *Advances in House-Tree-Person Techniques: Variations and Applications.* Los Angeles: Western Psychological Services. 1969.

BURNS, R. C. and KAUFMAN, S. H. *Kinetic Family Drawings (K-F-D): An Introduction to Understanding Children Through Kinetic Drawings.* New York: Brunner/Mazel. 1970.

BURNS, R. C. and KAUFMAN, S. H. *Actions, Styles and Symbols in Kinetic Family Drawings (K-F-D): An Interpretative Manual.* New York: Brunner/Mazel. 1972.

BURNS, R. C. *Self-Growth in Families: Kinetic Family Drawings (K-F-D) Research and Application.* New York: Brunner/Mazel. 1982

BURNS, R. C. *Kinetic-House-Tree-Person Drawings (K-H-T-P): An Interpretative Manual.* New York: Brunner/Mazel. 1987.

COWARD, H. *Jung and Eastern Thought.* New York: State Univ. of New York Press. 1985.

FREUD, S. *The Basic Writings of Sigmund Freud,* edited by A. A. Brill. New York: The Modern Library, Random House. 1938.

FURTH, G. M. *The Secret World Of Drawings.* Boston. Sigo Press. 1988.

GOODENOUGH, F. *Measurement of Intelligence by Drawings.* New York: Harcourt, Brace and World. 1926.

HAMMER, E. F. *The Clinical Application of Projective Drawings.* Springfield, IL: Charles C Thomas. 1980.

JUNG, C. G. *The Portable Jung.* New York: Pegasus Books. 1976.

JUNG, C. G. *Word and Image.* Bollingen Series XCVLL. Princeton, N.J.: Princeton Univ. Press. 1979.

JUNG, C. G. *The Collected Works. Vol. 12, Psychology and Alchemy.* Translated by R. F. C. Hull. London: Routledge & Kegan Paul, 1953.

JUNG, C. G. *The Collected Works. Vol. 9, part 1, The Archetypes and the Collective Unconscious.* Translated by R. F. C. Hull. Bollingen Series no. 20. Princeton, N.J., Princeton University Press, 1959.

JUNG, C. G. *The Collected Works. Vol. 16, The Practice of Psychotherapy.* Translated by R. F. C. Hull. Bollingen Series, no. 20. Princeton, N.J., Princeton University Press, 1966.

JUNG, C. G. *The Collected Works. Vol. 8, The Structure and the Dynamics of the Psyche.* Translated by R. F. C. Hull. Bollingen Series no. 20. Princeton, N.J., Princeton University Press, 1969.

MACHOVER, K. *Personality Projection in the Drawing of the Human Figure.* Springfield IL: Charles C Thomas. 1949.

MASLOW, A. H. *Motivation and Personality.* New York: Harper and Row. 1954.

MASLOW, A. H. *Toward a Psychology of Being.* New York: Van Nostrand. 1962.

MASLOW, A. H. *Religions, Values, and Peak Experiences.* Columbus, Ohio: Ohio State University Press. 1964.

METZNER, R. The tree as a symbol of self unfoldment. *The American Theosophist,* Fall. 1981.

REPS, P. *Zen Flesh, Zen Bones.* Rutland, Vermont: Charles E. Tuttle Co. 1957.

RICHARDS, M. C. *Centering.* Middletown, Conn.: Wesleyan University Press. 1962.

ROGERS, C. R. *On Becoming a Person.* Boston: Houghton Mifflen. 1963.

RORSCHACH, H. *Psychodiagnostics.* Berne: Verlag Hans Huber. 1942.

SCOON, R. *Greek Philosophy Before Plato.* Princeton, NJ: Princeton Univ. Press. 1928.

ADDITIONAL READINGS

ANNUNZIATA, J. An empirical investigation of the Kinetic Family Drawing of children of divorce and children from intact families. Rutgers University. Dissertation Abstracts International, 45, 342B. 1983.

ATKINSON, A. John's family in Kinetic Family Drawings. *The Commentary,* 1, 3. Carr Publishing Co., Bountiful, Utah. 1977.

BJOLGERUD, E. Children's view of the parents' roles in home and society as shown in their drawings. Masters thesis, University of Oslo. 1977.

BLOUNT, C. Changing family roles. Ph.D. dissertation. Seattle University. 1981.

BREWER, F. L. Children's interaction patterns in Kinetic Family Drawings. Dissertation Abstracts International. 41, 4253B. 1981.

BRITAIN, S. D. Effects of manipulation of children's affect on their family drawings. *Journal of Projective Techniques and Personality Assessments, 34,* 324-327. 1970.

BROWN, T. R. KFD in evaluating foster home care. Office of Research, State of Washington, Dept. of Social and Health Services. Olympia, WA. 1977.

BURNS, R. C. Kinetic Family Drawings. Practice and Research Panel. Annual Meeting, The American Association of Psychiatric Services for Children. Chicago. Taperecording. Audio Transcripts Ltd. New York, N.Y. 1979.

BURNS, R. C. What children are telling us in their human figure drawings. *Early Childhood Council, 11,* 3. Saskatchewan, Canada. 1980.

CHASE, D. A. An analysis of human figure and kinetic family drawings of sexually abused children of adolescents. Evanston Hospital, Ill. 1987.

CUMMINGS, J. A. An evaluation of an objective scoring system for kinetic family drawings. Doctoral dissertation, University of Georgia. Dissertation Abstracts International, 41, 2313B. 1980.

DEREN, S. An empirical evaluation of the validity of a Draw-A-Family Test. *Journal of Clinical Psychology, 31,* 542-546. 1975.

DILEO, J. H. *Children's Drawings as Diagnostic Aids.* Brunner/Mazel, New York. 1973.

FREEMAN, H. What a child's drawings can reveal. *Mother, 35,* 34-36. London. July, 1971.

HEINEMAN, T. Kinetic family drawings of siblings of severely emotionally disturbed children. Thesis Abstracts. School of Social Welfare. University of California at Berkeley. 1975.

HOLMQUIST, J. Anthropological K-F-D study of Pasqualian families on Pasqua (Easter Island). Ph.D. dissertation. Dept. of Anthropology, University of California, Berkeley. 1972.

HOLMQUIST, U. Children draw their families; A Swedish handbook for diagnosis of children based on the Kinetic Family Drawing techniques by Burns and Kaufman. Masters thesis, University of Gothenburg, Sweden. 1987.

HOLTZ, R., BRANNIGAN, G. G. & SCHOFIELD, J. J. The kinetic family drawing as a measure of interpersonal distance. *Journal of Genetic Psychology, 137,* 307-308. 1980.

HOWITT, P. S. Kinetic family drawings and clinical judgment: An evaluation of judges' ability to differentiate between the K-F-D's of abusing, controlling and concerned mothers. Dissertation Abstracts International, 45, 1289B (University Microfilms No. 05-54,194). 1978.

HULSE, W. C. The emotionally disturbed child draws his family. *Quarterly Journal of Child Behavior.* 3:152-174. 1951.

JACOBSON, D. A. A study of Kinetic Family Drawings of public school children ages six through nine. University of Cincinnati. Dissertation Abstracts International. Order #73-29-455. 1974.

JOHNSON, D. D. Comparison on DAF and K-F-D in children from intact and divorced homes. Thesis Abstracts. California State University, San Jose, 1975.

JORDAN, S. J. A validity study of Kinetic Family Drawings. Dissertation. Texas Women's University. 1985.

KATO, T., IKURA, H. & KUBO, Y. A study on the "style" in kinetic family drawing. *Japanese Bulletin of Art Therapy, 7,* 1976.

KATO, T. & SHIMIZU, T. The action of K-F-D and the child's attitude towards family members. *Japanese Bulletin for Art Therapy, 9,* 1978.

KATO, T. Pictorial expression of family relations in young children. 1X International Congress of Psychopathology of Expression. Verona, Italy. 1979.

KLEPSCH, M. & LOGIE, L. *Children Draw and Tell.* Brunner/Mazel, New York. 1982.

KNOFF, H. M. & PROUT, H. The kinetic drawing system: A review and integration of kinetic family and school drawing techniques. *Psychology in Schools 22,* 1. 1985.

KNOFF, H. M. & PROUT, H. *The Kinetic Drawing System—Family and School: A Handbook.* Los Angeles. Western Psychological Services. 1985.

KOPPITZ, E. M. *Psychological Evaluation of Children's Human Figure Drawing.* Grune and Stratton. New York. 1968.

LANDMARK, M. K-F-D's in Norway. Institute of Psychology, University of Oslo, Norway. Communication with R. C. Burns.

LAYTON, M. C. Specific features in the kinetic family drawings of children. Dissertation Abstracts International. 45, 356B. University Microfilms No. 84-10, 204. 1981.

LEDESMA, L. K. The kinetic family drawings of Filipino adolescents. Dissertation Abstracts International, 40 1866B. University Microfilms No. 22, 79, 072. 1979.

LEVENBERG, S. B. Professional training, psychodiagnostic skill and Kinetic Family Drawings. *Journal of Personality Assessment.* August 1975.

LOWERY, C. R., ROSS, E. & MCGREGOR, P. The Kinetic Family Drawing. Paper. 31st Annual Meeting of American Association of Psychiatric Services for Children. Chicago, IL. November 1979.

MACHOVER, K. *Personality Projection in the Drawing of the Human Figure.* Springfield IL: Charles C Thomas. 1949.

MANGUM, M. E. Familial identification in black, anglo, and chicano MR children using K-F-D. Dissertation Abstracts International. 36 (11-A), 7343. 1976.

MCCALLISTER, R. Usefulness of the Kinetic Family Drawing in the assessment of aggression among a population of juvenile offenders. Doctoral dissertation, Auburn University. Dissertation Abstracts International. 44, 2252B. 1983.

MCDONALD, M. Relationship between father/daughter incest as manifest in K-F-Ds of adolescent girls. Thesis: Antioch University, San Francisco. 1980.

MCGREGOR, J. Kinetic Family Drawing test: A validity study. Dissertation Abstracts International, 40, 927B-928B (University Microfilms No. 7918101) 1978.

MCNAUGHTON, E. Developmental aspects of K-F-D's in children. Houston, Texas. Communication with R. C. Burns.

MEI MEI CHO. Validity of the K-F-D as a measure of self concept and parent/child relationships among Chinese children in Taiwan. Dissertation. Andrews University. 1987.

MENTOR, J. Values clarification through art forms: A projective technique. M.A. thesis, San Francisco Theological Seminary. 1981.

MEYERS, D. V. Toward an objective evaluation of the kinetic family drawing (KFD). *Journal of Personality Assessment, 42,* 358-365. 1978.

MOSTKOFF, D. L. & LAZURUS, P. J. The Kinetic Family Drawing: The reliability of an objective scoring system. *Psychology in Schools, 20,* 16-20. 1983.

O'BRIEN, R. O. & PATTON, W. F. Development of an object scoring method for the kinetic family drawing. *Journal of Personality Assessment,* 156-64. 1974.

OGDON, D. P. *Handbook of Psychological Signs, Symptoms and Syndromes.* Los Angeles, Western Psychological Services. 1982.

PETERSEN, C. S. Roots: As shown in Kinetic Family Drawings. *The Commentary,* Vol. 1, No. 3, Carr Publishing Co., Bountiful, Utah. 1977.

PROUT, H. T. & CELMER, D. S. School drawings and academic achievement: A validity study of the kinetic school drawing technique. *Psychology in the Schools, 21,* 176-180. 1984.

PURYEAR, D. L. Familial experiences: A comparison between the children of lesbian mothers and the children of heterosexual mothers. Dissertation Abstracts International. 44, 3941B. University Microfilms No. 84-03, 829. 1984.

RASKIN, L. M. & BLOOM, A. S. Kinetic family drawings by children with learning disabilities. *Journal of Pediatric Psychology, 4,* 247-251. 1979.

RASKIN, L. M. & PITCHER, G. B. Kinetic family drawings by children with perceptual-motor delays. *Journal of Learning Disabilities, 10,* 370-374. 1977.

REYNOLDS, C. R. A quick scoring guide to the interpretation of children's kinetic family drawings. *Psychology in the Schools, 15,* 489-492. 1978.

RHINE, P. C. Adjustment indicators in the kinetic family drawing by children: A validation study. Dissertation Abstracts International, 39 2B, 955. 1978.

ROTH, J. W. & HUBER, B. L. *Kinetic Family Drawings. Familien Dynamik, Soderdruck.* Stuttgart: Klett-Cotta. 1979.

SARBAUGH, M. E. *Kinetic-Drawing-School Technique.* Illinois School Psychologist's Association Monograph Series, 1, 1-70. 1982.

SAYED, A. J. & LEAVERTON, D. R. Kinetic family drawings of children with diabetes. *Child Psychiatry and Human Development, 5,* 40-50. 1974.

SCHILDKRAUT, M. S., SHENDER, I. R. & SONNENBLICK, M. *Human Figure Drawings in Adolescents.* Brunner/Mazel, New York. 1972.

SCHNEIDER, G. B. A preliminary validation study of the kinetic school drawing. Dissertation Abstracts International, 38, 6228A. University Microfilms No. 7805520. 1978.

SCHORNSTEIN, H. M. & DERR, J. The many applications of kinetic family drawings in child abuse. *British Journal of Projective Psychology and Personality Study, 23,* 33-35. 1978.

SHEAR, C. R. & RUSSELL, K. R. Use of the family drawing as a technique for studying parent/child interaction. *Journal of Projective Techniques and Personality Assessments, 33,* 1. 1969.

SIMS, C. A. Kinetic family drawings and the family relations indicator. *Journal of Clinical Psychology,* 30, 87-88. 1974.

SMOOTE, S. D. K-F-D's in an institutionalized delinquent population with a history of child abuse. Part of dissertation. Texas A & M University. College of Education. 1986.

SOBEL, M. & SOBEL, W. Discriminating adolescent male delinquents through the use of kinetic family drawings. *Journal of Personality Assessment, 40,* 91-94. 1976.

SOUZA DE JOODE, M. O Desenho Cinetico da Familia (KFD) como instrumento de diagnostico da dinamica do relacionamento familiar. [The Kinetic Family Drawing (K-F-D) as a diagnostic instrument for family dynamics and relationships.] *Auguivos Brasileiros de Psicologia Aplicada, 29,* 149-162. 1976.

THOMPSON, L. V. Kinetic family drawings of adolescents. Dissertation Abstracts International, 36, 3077B-3078B. 1975.

WORDEN, M. A case study comparison of Draw-A-Person and Kinetic Family Drawing. *Journal of Personality Assessment, 49,* 4, 427-433. 1985.

YOUNGER, R. B. Psychology and the kinetic drawing. Doctoral dissertation, Auburn University. Dissertation Abstracts International, 43, 3382B. 1982.